ICELAND TRAVEL GUIDE 2023 - 2024

The Ideal Vacation Guide To Iceland: Unlock The Hidden Gems Of The Nomadic Island's Paradise With Complete Essential Tips For First Time Visitors

BY

WILLIAM JOSE

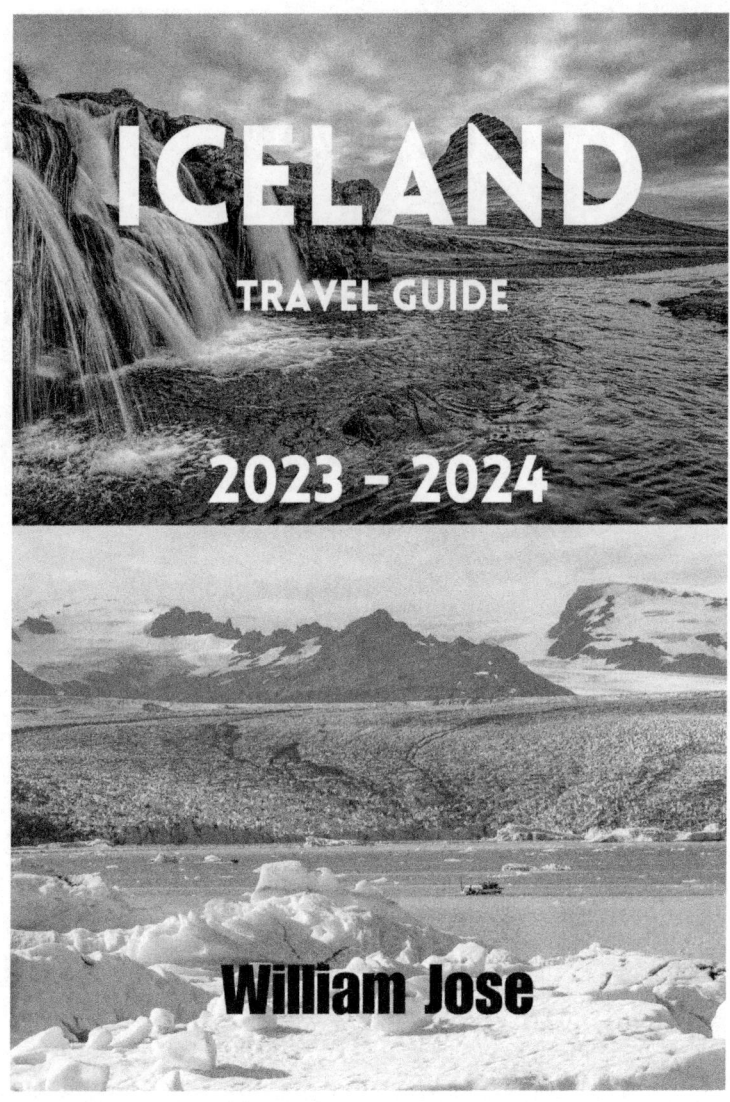

All rights reserved. No part of this publication may be reproduced, distributed, or transmitted in any form or by any means, including photocopying, recording, or other electronic or mechanical methods, without the prior written permission of the publisher, except in the case of brief quotations embodied in critical reviews and certain other noncommercial uses permitted by copyright law.

Copyright © William Jose , 2023

TABLE OF CONTENTS

TABLE OF CONTENTS.. 4
INTRODUCTION.. 7
A Brief History of Iceland.. 9
Iceland's Population.. 12
Icelandic Religious Practice...................................... 12

Chapter One.. 14
Getting To Iceland, The Nomadic Island's Paradise 14
Air Travel To Iceland... 15
Land Travel To Iceland.. 16
Sea Travel to Iceland.. 18
Month by Month Weather in Iceland........................ 19
January - February... 19
March - April... 20
May - June.. 20
July - August... 21
September - October.. 21
November - December... 22
Best Times To Visit Iceland...................................... 23

Chapter Two.. 25
Iceland Travel Planning And Exploration................. 25
The Neighborhoods Region of Iceland..................... 25
Iceland's Capital City Tour.. 28
Transit Options of Exploring Iceland Neighborhood Cities.. 30

Icelandic Entry Requirements......................32
Iceland Tourist Stay Durations...................33
Iceland Travel Essentials...........................34

Chapter Three...36
Top Attractions and Recreational Activities in Iceland..36
Top Attractions in Iceland...........................36
Who Should Visit Iceland?.........................39
Best Adventure Activities..........................42
Festivals & Events that Shouldn't Be Missed.........45
Top Tourist Cities to Stay In Iceland.........47

Chapter Four...50
Eco-Friendly Hotels & Resorts With Their Prices Rates...50
Budget Friendly Tourist Hotels & Resorts...............52
Luxury Tourist Hotels and Resorts............53
Vacation Rentals and Apartments.............55
Iceland Hostels and Guesthouse...............57
Iceland Tourist Camp Venues....................59

Chapter Five...61
Historical Monuments And Icelandic Heritage........61
Contemporary Art Galleries And Museums............64
National Parks And Reserve.......................66
Gardens and Romantic Couples Packs....68
Zoos And Educational Museums...............71
Chapter Six..73

Iceland's Nightlife At A Glance....................73
A Guide To Iceland Active Bars and Nightclubs...... 74
How to Locate Live Music Venues and Jazz Clubs. 76
Jazz And live Music Venues.......................... 78
Tips for A Memorable Night in Iceland..................... 80

Chapter Seven................ 86
Iceland Food And Drinks........................... 86
Favorite Food & Cuisines.......................... 86
Favorite Drinks in Iceland........................... 89
Vegan and Vegetarian Options..................... 90
Best Cafes & Restaurants in Iceland....................... 92
Icelandic Dining Etiquette........................95

Chapter Eight................98
What To Know Before Traveling To Iceland............. 98
The Icelandic currency................................98
Money Exchange Spot in Iceland............................99
LGBTQ + Acceptance................................ 101
Emergency Contacts.................................103
Iceland Cultural Etiquette........................... 104

Chapter Nine................ 108
Iceland Sustainable Budget Travel......................... 108
Top Money Saving Strategies....................108
Bargaining and Negotiation Strategies...................111
Iceland's Top Budget Markets................... 113
Chapter Ten................ 116

6

Goodbye, Iceland..116
Favorite Travel Souvenirs in Iceland....................... 116
Safety Tips For First-Time Visitors.......................... 118
Helpful Websites and Bookings Resources........... 121
Conclusion... 123

INTRODUCTION

Iceland, sometimes known as the "Land of Fire and Ice," is an enthralling Nordic island nation in the North Atlantic Ocean. Iceland has been an increasingly popular tourist destination due to its magnificent scenery, geothermal marvels, and rich cultural history. Iceland, with an area of around 103,000 square kilometers, is famed for its breathtaking natural beauty. The terrain is dominated by vast glaciers, gushing waterfalls, rough lava fields, and volcanic mountains, creating a unique and scenic atmosphere. The region also has a plethora of geothermal hot springs, including the famed Blue Lagoon, where tourists may relax in peaceful thermal pools surrounded by a strange volcanic landscape.

The geology of Iceland is determined by its location on the Mid-Atlantic Ridge, a tectonic barrier between the Eurasian and North American plates. Geysers, where hot water bursts from the earth, and the beautiful Gullfoss waterfall are the consequence of this geological activity. The country is also renowned for its volcanoes, particularly Eyjafjallajökull, whose eruption in 2010 drew worldwide attention.

The capital city, Reykjavik, has a blend of contemporary and traditional attractions. Visitors may stroll through the city's picturesque streets, see the historic Hallgrimskirkja Church, and sample the vibrant nightlife and unique food.

Icelandic culture is firmly steeped in Norse myths and customs. The sagas, or old Icelandic literary works, provide witness to the country's rich history. Many Old Norse characteristics have been preserved in Icelandic, making it intriguing to linguists and language aficionados. The fauna on the island is another draw, with several bird species, including puffins, breeding along the cliffs. Iceland's waterways are filled with marine life, making whale-watching trips a popular activity.

Iceland's dedication to environmental sustainability is notable. The nation is a worldwide pioneer in green projects due to its reliance on renewable energy sources such as geothermal and hydroelectric electricity. Iceland provides a totally unique experience, whether you're looking for breathtaking vistas, cultural discovery, or a connection with nature. From its geothermal marvels to its rich cultural past, this Nordic jewel never ceases to wow tourists with its natural beauty and kind welcome.

A Brief History of Iceland

Iceland, a Nordic island country in the North Atlantic Ocean, has a rich and intriguing history spanning over a thousand years. The earliest permanent settlements on the island were created in the 9th century by Norse immigrants, mostly from Norway.

Early in Icelandic history, a decentralized chieftain system was established, with various separate chieftains dominating different sections of the island. The Commonwealth period, which lasted until the 13th century, was named as such. During this period, Iceland evolved a distinct legal and political system known as the Althing, which was one of the world's first legislative institutions. Through a series of intricate political events in the 13th century, Iceland fell under the sovereignty of Norway and then Denmark. Because it reduced Iceland's sovereignty and established Lutheranism as the main religion, Danish authority had a considerable influence on Icelandic society and culture.

Iceland had several challenges throughout the 18th and 19th centuries. For most of its people, the island faced economic stagnation and horrible living circumstances. A national awakening, however, occurred in the late nineteenth century, fueled by revived interest in Icelandic literature, culture, and language. This cultural rebirth helped pave the way for Iceland's independence struggle.

Iceland obtained some autonomy from Denmark in 1904 and progressively progressed toward complete independence. Iceland gained its long-desired independence and became a republic on June 17, 1944. The nation saw significant social and economic growth after WWII, powered by its fishing sector and, subsequently, tourist boom.

The eruption of the volcano Eyjafjallajökull in 2010 was also a significant event in Iceland's history. The eruption caused flight disruptions throughout Europe and drew international attention to Iceland's natural beauties and geological activity.

Iceland has been well-known in recent years for its dedication to environmental sustainability and renewable energy sources. The country makes use of its enormous geothermal and hydroelectric resources, making it one of the world's greenest countries.

Iceland is today recognized for its magnificent landscapes, geysers, hot springs, and spectacular waterfalls, which draw people from all over the globe. It boasts a vibrant artistic and cultural environment, and its residents have a good level of life. Iceland continues to catch the imagination and make a lasting effect on those who come due to its unique history, natural beauty, and hardy people.

Iceland's Population

The population of Iceland is minimal. It has been estimated in recent years to be approximately 366,000 individuals. It is crucial to remember, however, that the population of Iceland in previous centuries, such as the 1500s, was substantially less. Iceland was sparsely inhabited at the time and faced a variety of obstacles, including natural catastrophes, disease epidemics, and severe living circumstances. According to historical documents, Iceland's population in the 16th century was believed to be between 40,000 and 60,000 people. This figure shifted as a result of causes such as famine, plagues, and emigration. Iceland's population has grown throughout the ages, although it remains small in comparison to many other nations across the globe.

Icelandic Religious Practice

Iceland has a distinct religious landscape that has developed through time. Iceland's primary religion is Lutheranism, especially the Evangelical Lutheran Church of Iceland, which serves as the country's national church. The church has always been an important part of Icelandic life and culture.

Iceland was formerly populated by Norse pagans who worship Norse gods such as Odin, Thor, and Freyja. Conversion to Christianity, however, started in the 10th century, and by the year 1000, Christianity had been formally recognized as Iceland's religion.

Today, the Evangelical Lutheran Church is the biggest Christian denomination in Iceland, with the majority of Icelanders identifying as Christians. However, in recent years, Iceland's religious landscape has grown increasingly diversified. Along with Christianity, there has been a rising secularization tendency in Iceland, with a sizable proportion of the population identifying as non-religious or agnostic. As a result of this transformation, religious practice and participation in conventional church rites has declined.

In addition to Christianity and secularism, Iceland has a number of minor religious groups. Other Christian faiths such as Catholicism, Pentecostalism, and different Protestant sects are included. Other faiths, such as Islam, Buddhism, and Paganism, have a modest but rising presence.

It should be noted that Iceland is recognized for its open and tolerant views toward religious beliefs. Religious freedom is legally guaranteed, and people are typically allowed to practice their beliefs without substantial limitations. In Icelandic society, interfaith discussion and cooperation are also promoted.

While Christianity, especially Lutheranism, is the dominant religion in Iceland, the nation has recently experienced a surge in secularism and a growing variety of religious views and practices.

Chapter One

Getting To Iceland, The Nomadic Island's Paradise

Iceland travel is an exciting and fascinating experience. Iceland, often known as the "Land of Fire and Ice," has a unique and stunning natural scenery that will take your breath away.

Air Travel To Iceland

Iceland is a renowned tourist destination known for its breathtaking landscapes, natural marvels, and one-of-a-kind experiences. Air travel is the most prevalent method of reaching Iceland from many areas across the globe. Please keep in mind that the information presented here is based on general knowledge, and it's always best to verify with airlines or travel agents for the most up-to-date and accurate flight and pricing information.

North Americans:

Several airlines provide direct flights from New York City (JFK) to Keflavik International Airport (KEF) in Iceland. The flight lasts around 5-6 hours and costs between $300 and $800 USD, depending on the season and availability.

Direct flights from Toronto Pearson International Airport (YYZ) to Keflavik International Airport (KEF) are available. The flight lasts around 6-7 hours and costs between $400 and $900 USD.

<u>From the continent of Europe</u>:
Many airlines fly straight from London airports (Heathrow, Gatwick, and Luton) to Keflavik International Airport (KEF). The flight lasts around three hours, and tickets vary from £100 to £300 GBP.

Direct flights are available from Berlin airports (Tegel and Schönefeld) to Keflavik International Airport (KEF). The flight lasts roughly 3-4 hours and costs between €150 to €400 EUR.

Flight rates may vary greatly based on variables such as the time of year, buying time in advance, airline discounts, and availability.

Land Travel To Iceland

To get to Iceland by car, you have two options: drive or take a boat. Let's look at other driving possibilities and their estimated costs:

Driving:
Personal Vehicle: If you possess a car, you may travel to Iceland via boat from continental Europe. The most popular route is with the ferry firm Smyril Line from Denmark (Hirtshals) to Iceland (Seyisfjörur). The cost of a one-way journey varies based on the season, vehicle type, and extra amenities. Prices for a single car (with driver) without a cabin varied from €300 to €1,500 as of my knowledge cutoff in September 2021.

Another alternative is to hire a vehicle in Europe and bring it on the boat. Rental vehicle businesses that enable cross-border travel to Iceland may be found, but be sure to read the terms and conditions carefully as extra costs may apply. The cost of a rental automobile is determined by the kind of vehicle, the length of the rental, and the business you pick. Rental automobiles in Europe may cost between €20 and €100 per day, not including ferry fees.

If you wish to go to Iceland from continental Europe, you may take a road journey across multiple countries, finally arriving in Denmark or another ferry departure point. The expenditures connected with this option would include gasoline, tolls, lodging, and any car maintenance required.

Sea Travel to Iceland

The cost of sea travel to Iceland varies based on criteria such as departure port, journey route, season, and mode of transportation. It's worth noting that water travel to Iceland is less prevalent than air travel, and your alternatives may be restricted. However, there are a few options worth considering:

Cruise Lines:
Departure Ports: Most cruise ships to Iceland leave from ports in the United Kingdom, Norway, or continental Europe.
Costs of cruise ship travel to Iceland may vary greatly based on the length of the journey, the facilities supplied, and the time of year. A regular 7-10 day trip might cost between $1,500 and $5,000 per person.
Ferries:

Departure Ports: There are only a few ferry routes to Iceland that leave from ports in Denmark or the Faroe Islands.

Costs vary based on the season and the kind of cabin or seats you choose. A one-way vacation may cost between $200 and $500 per person on average.

It should be noted that water transport to Iceland is weather-dependent and may have limited availability, especially during the winter months. For the most up-to-date information on routes, timetables, and fees, it is best to contact particular cruise lines or ferry operators.

However, it's worth noting that flight travel is the most popular and convenient way to go to Iceland. Several airlines fly to Iceland on a regular basis from different areas across the globe, allowing greater flexibility and perhaps more inexpensive choices than sea travel.

Month by Month Weather in Iceland

Iceland dances through the seasons, from glacial beauty to blazing sky, an ever-changing symphony of weather. Each month has its own unique story to tell, painting the landscape with its own palette of materials.

January - February

Iceland's winter season lasts from January to February, and it is marked by low temperatures and unpredictable weather. Temperatures in coastal regions vary from -1°C to 3°C (30°F to 37°F), while temperatures in the interior may fall below freezing. Snowfall is frequent, blanketing the countryside in a beautiful white blanket. Strong gusts are common, especially around the coast, adding to the cold. The days are short, with just a few hours of sun, while the nights are lengthy. It's a period when the enthralling beauty of Iceland's glacial landscapes is enhanced, allowing for winter sports like skiing, snowboarding, and exploring ice caves.

March - April

In March and April, Iceland transitions from winter to spring. During this time, the weather may be extremely unpredictable. Temperatures will be cold, ranging from 0°C to 5°C (32°F to 41°F), with snowfall possible. However, with more sunshine and a steady rise in temperatures, there are hints of spring. Pack warm clothes and be prepared for changing weather conditions if you want to visit Iceland in March or April.

May - June

Iceland has temperate and pleasant weather in May and June, with extended daylight hours. Temperatures in May vary from 7°C to 13°C (45°F to 55°F) and rise to 10°C to 15°C (50°F to 59°F) in June. As spring flowers around the nation, visitors may anticipate a mix of sunny days and occasional showers, as well as breathtaking scenery.

July - August

July and August are prime summer months in Iceland, with pleasant temperatures and reasonably consistent meteorological conditions. Temperatures typically vary from 10 to 15 degrees Celsius (50 to 59 degrees Fahrenheit), with highs sometimes reaching 20 degrees Celsius (68 degrees Fahrenheit). These months have extended daylight hours, with some sections of the nation seeing almost 24 hours of daylight. It is crucial to know, however, that weather in Iceland may be unpredictable, with quick variations.

September - October

Iceland transitions from summer to autumn between September and October. The weather is pleasant, with temperatures ranging from 5°C to 12°C (41°F to 54°F). Throughout these months, the days get shorter and the risk of rain increases. When traveling, it is best to bring warm and waterproof gear since weather conditions might change quickly. It's a lovely time to see Iceland's breathtaking landscapes covered with fall hues.

November - December

Winter arrives in Iceland between November and December, bringing cooler temperatures and fewer daylight hours. In November, average temperatures vary from roughly -1°C to 3°C (30°F to 37°F), declining to -2°C to 2°C (28°F to 36°F) in December. Snowfall becomes more common, particularly at higher altitudes and in the north. Daylight hours are drastically reduced, with just a few hours of sunlight each day, while dark evenings rule the landscape. Strong gusts and storms are possible, adding to the wintry atmosphere. Visitors may view breathtaking winter landscapes, frozen waterfalls, and the mesmerizing Northern Lights dance across the sky, making it a fantastic time to visit Iceland.

Winter arrives in Iceland between November and December, bringing cooler temperatures and fewer daylight hours. In November, average temperatures vary from roughly -1°C to 3°C (30°F to 37°F), declining to -2°C to 2°C (28°F to 36°F) in December. Snowfall becomes more common, particularly at higher altitudes and in the north. Daylight hours are drastically reduced, with just a few hours of sunlight each day, while dark evenings rule the landscape. Strong gusts and storms are possible, adding to the wintry atmosphere. Visitors may view breathtaking winter landscapes, frozen waterfalls, and the mesmerizing Northern Lights dance across the sky, making it a fantastic time to visit Iceland.

Best Times To Visit Iceland

The ideal time to visit Iceland is primarily determined by your own choices and the experiences you intend to have during your trip. Iceland is a nation of spectacular landscapes, breathtaking natural beauty, and one-of-a-kind geological marvels. Here's a seasonal breakdown to help you decide:

Summer (June to August): Due to the better weather and extended daylight hours, as well as the legendary midnight sun, this is Iceland's busiest tourist season. The landscape is colorful and accessible, with chances for hiking, glacier exploration, and other outdoor activities. It's also an excellent time for bird and whale viewing.

Winter (December to February): Winter in Iceland is an entirely unique experience. Despite the decreased daylight hours, the fascinating Northern Lights may be seen moving across the dark sky. It's the season for snowy vistas, ice caves, and winter activities like skiing and snowboarding. During this time, the iconic Golden Circle attractions are less crowded.

Shoulder seasons (spring and autumn): These transitional seasons, which last from March to May and September to November, provide a variety of benefits. Fewer visitors, reduced rates, and greater availability are possible while still enjoying some excellent weather conditions. Landscapes are often ornamented with vibrant fall leaves or blooming flora in the spring.

Finally, the optimal time to visit Iceland is determined by your interests and the kind of experience you are looking for. Consider your favorite activities, weather preferences, and the amount of tourist crowds while deciding on a season.

Chapter Two

Iceland Travel Planning And Exploration

Prepare to be fascinated by the kingdom of fire and ice, where natural marvels abound. Iceland entices with its mystical vistas and breathtaking splendor. As a visitor, embrace the spirit of exploration and immerse yourself in the wonder that awaits you. But keep in mind that Iceland's attractiveness is only equaled by its wild environment, so bring sturdy footwear, an adventurous attitude, and an open heart. Iceland provides a kaleidoscope of experiences that will leave you breathless, from gushing waterfalls to hot geysers, black sand beaches to glistening glaciers. So pack your curiosity, wanderlust, and a camera, for the trip of a lifetime awaits you in this region of boundless wonder.

The Neighborhoods Region of Iceland

Despite its tiny size, Iceland boasts a number of towns and cities that provide distinct attractions and experiences. Here are some of Iceland's most significant neighborhoods and cities, along with their attractions:

Reykjavik:
Iceland's capital and biggest city is Reykjavik. It is well-known for its dynamic cultural scene, colorful architecture, and active nightlife. Reykjavik's attractions include:
Hallgrimskirkja: A beautiful church with a unique design and panoramic views from its tower.
The Harpa Concert Hall is a contemporary architectural marvel that holds concerts, exhibits, and plays.
The Sun Voyager: A captivating sculpture of a Viking ship found near the shoreline.
The National Museum of Iceland provides information on Iceland's history, culture, and legacy.
Laugavegur is the major shopping strip in Iceland, packed with stores, boutiques, cafés, and restaurants.

Akureyri:
Akureyri is Iceland's second-largest city, situated in the north. It is well-known for its scenic scenery and outdoor sports. Akureyri's attractions include:
Akureyri Botanical Garden: A tranquil garden with a vast range of flora and flowers.

The Akureyri Church is a remarkable structure with panoramic views of the city and neighboring mountains.
Christmas House: A Christmas-themed business open all year with decorations, presents, and a festive ambiance.
Hof Cultural and Conference Center: A contemporary cultural center that hosts a variety of events and exhibits.
Tours for whale viewing: Akureyri is a popular starting place for whale watching excursions in the surrounding seas.

Vik:
Vik is a lovely hamlet on Iceland's south coast. It is well-known for its spectacular scenery, black sand beaches, and closeness to major natural features. Vik's attractions include:
Reynisfjara Beach: A beautiful black sand beach with unusual basalt column formations and spectacular cliffs.
Reynisdrangar: Folklore and Viking stories surround the basalt sea stacks at Reynisfjara Beach.
Dyrhólaey is a spectacular promontory with a lighthouse and a massive natural arch.
Skógafoss: A spectacular waterfall with a 60-meter plunge that offers trekking and photographic possibilities.
Mrdalsjökull Glacier: An ice cap that covers the active Katla volcano, with glacier trekking and snowmobile trips available.

Akranes:

Akranes is a town situated on Iceland's west coast. It has both natural beauty and cultural attractions. Akranes' attractions include:

Akranes Lighthouse: A beautiful lighthouse with stunning views of the surrounding shoreline.

Langisandur Beach: A lovely sandy beach recognized for its peace and beauty.

Akranes Folk Museum: Akranes' history, traditional Icelandic culture, and artifacts are on display.

Gardar BA 64: A beached ship that may be visited and photographed.

Glymur Waterfall: This neighboring waterfall is Iceland's second-tallest, tumbling down a scenic canyon.

These are only a few examples of Icelandic neighborhoods and cities, each with its own distinct charms and charm. Exploring several parts of the nation enables tourists to discover Iceland's unique landscapes, cultural legacy, and natural marvels.

Iceland's Capital City Tour

Reykjavik, Iceland's capital city, is recognized for its breathtaking landscapes, natural treasures, and bustling cities. Let's take a virtual tour of the city's most important districts and attractions.

Downtown Reykjavik: The city's center, with its colorful buildings, beautiful streets, and bustling atmosphere. There are various businesses, restaurants, cafés, and pubs in this area. Laugavegur, the main street, is a famous shopping and eating destination.

The Old Reykjavik area is located west of downtown and is the city's historic district. It is known for its well-preserved wooden buildings, winding alleyways, and attractions like the Reykjavik Cathedral (Hallgrmskirkja) and the Parliament House (Alingi).

The Harbor region: The harbor region, located close downtown, is a lively spot with a mix of fishing boats, whale watching trips, and bright seafood restaurants. The renowned Harpa Concert Hall, a contemporary architectural wonder, is also located here.

Vesturbaer: Vesturbaer is a residential neighborhood with a laid-back attitude located west of downtown. It's a lovely area for a stroll, with gorgeous parks, the University of Iceland campus, and the Reykjavik City Museum nearby.

Laugardalur: Located east of downtown, Laugardalur is a leisure district famed for its green areas. It is home to the Laugardalslaug, Reykjavik's biggest swimming pool complex, as well as botanical gardens, sports facilities, and the renowned Reykjavik Zoo.

Hlar: Hlar is a residential area south of downtown with a mix of new and older homes. It's a more peaceful neighborhood with attractions including the Kringlan shopping mall, the famous Reykjavik Park and Zoo, and the Perlan building with its observation deck.

These are only a few highlights of the neighborhoods of Reykjavik. Reykjavik is a city worth visiting on foot or by bike since each region has its own distinct charm and attractions. During your vacation, don't forget to try the local food and immerse yourself in Iceland's lively culture.

Transit Options of Exploring Iceland Neighborhood Cities

There are various modes of transportation accessible for touring Iceland's towns and cities. Here are some typical modes of transportation to consider while touring Iceland Neighborhoods, as well as their prices.

Public Bus: Public buses are provided in Iceland's main towns and cities, including Reykjavik. Strtó operates the public bus system, which provides dependable and economical transportation. Prices vary based on distance traveled, but a single ride inside Reykjavik normally costs between 440 and 550 Icelandic króna (ISK), or $3.50 and $4.50 USD.

Taxis: Taxis are widely accessible in Iceland, especially in metropolitan areas. They make it easy and pleasant to explore communities. Taxis in Iceland are metered, with charges varying somewhat depending on the taxi provider. The initial charge is generally about 800-900 ISK (about $6.50-$7.50 USD), and the cost each kilometer is around 250-350 ISK (about $2-$3 USD).

Rental Cars: Renting a vehicle is a popular way to explore the neighborhoods of Iceland, particularly in more distant locations where public transit may be restricted. The cost of renting a vehicle varies based on the automobile model, rental period, and rental operator. A compact budget automobile may cost between 7,000 and 12,000 ISK (roughly $57 and $98 USD) each day.

Bicycles: Bicycles may be hired in some locations of Iceland, mainly in Reykjavik and other tourist destinations. Bicycle rentals vary in price, but you should budget roughly 2,000-3,500 ISK (around $16-$28 USD) each day.

Walking: Walking is an excellent method to discover neighborhoods, particularly in densely populated cities. It is free and enables you to explore the area at your own speed. The majority of Iceland's neighborhoods are pedestrian-friendly, with sidewalks and designated walking pathways.

Please keep in mind that these are estimates and might change based on the season, location, and individual rental businesses or taxi services. For the most up-to-date information on transport choices and prices in Iceland, always check with local companies or websites.

Icelandic Entry Requirements

The following are the entrance criteria for Iceland.

Passport: All travelers visiting Iceland must have a valid passport that is valid for at least three months beyond the date of their anticipated departure.

The visa requirements for Iceland vary depending on your nationality. For stays of up to 90 days within a 180-day period, citizens of the European Union (EU) and European Economic Area (EEA), as well as many other nations, do not need a visa. If you are from a visa-required nation, you will need to get a Schengen visa before visiting Iceland.

Iceland Tourist Stay Durations

The length of your stay in Iceland as a tourist will depend on your particular interests, budget, and amount of time available. Most tourists, however, feel that a stay of 7 to 10 days provides for a thorough exploration of the country's principal attractions and natural treasures.

When planning your journey, keep in mind that changing weather and road conditions might alter travel times and accessibility to some places. Furthermore, Iceland's prime tourist season is from June to August, so availability and costs may vary depending on when you visit.

Iceland Travel Essentials

When visiting Iceland as a tourist, it is important to prepare correctly for the country's distinctive temperature and different scenery. Here are some key things to consider adding to your packing list:

Clothing:
Waterproof and windproof jacket: Because Iceland's weather is unpredictable, a robust, waterproof jacket with a hood is required.

Pack a variety of lightweight, breathable layers like long-sleeved shirts, sweaters, and thermal base layers. This helps you to adapt to changing weather conditions.

Warm, waterproof trousers: For outdoor activities, consider carrying waterproof pants or thermal leggings.

Sturdy, waterproof hiking boots: For exploring Iceland's harsh landscape, you'll need comfortable, waterproof footwear with decent grip.

Keep your head, hands, and neck warm with a hat, gloves, and scarf, particularly if you're traveling during the cooler months.

Outdoor Equipment:
Backpack: A sturdy backpack with a rain cover is ideal for day excursions and hiking.
Binoculars: Great for bird watching and seeing the beautiful scenery from a distance.
Sunglasses and sunscreen: Even in the colder months, the reflected sunshine from snow and ice may be powerful.

Electronics:
Consider carrying a camera to record the amazing views that Iceland has to offer.
Iceland utilizes Type C and Type F plugs, so make sure you have the correct adaptor for your equipment.

Miscellaneous:
Bring a swimsuit if you want to relax in Iceland's geothermal hot springs and pools.
A small, quick-drying towel is great for swimming or visiting hot springs.
prescriptions: Bring any prescription prescriptions you may need, as well as a small first-aid kit.
Reusable water bottle: Because Iceland's tap water is pure and safe, a reusable water bottle will help you keep hydrated.
Good luck with your Iceland travel planning.

Chapter Three

Top Attractions and Recreational Activities in Iceland

Every explorer will find a world of wonder in this Nordic island kingdom. Iceland's best attractions will leave you speechless, whether you're enthralled by gushing waterfalls, charmed by volcanic vistas, or captured by the otherworldly Northern Lights. And when it comes to recreational activities, Iceland promises to inspire your sense of adventure like no other location on Earth, whether it's exploring ice caves, trekking glaciers, relaxing in geothermal hot springs, or going on exciting whale-watching expeditions.

Top Attractions in Iceland

Iceland is well-known for its breathtaking natural scenery and one-of-a-kind attractions. Here are some of Iceland's greatest attractions:

The Blue Lagoon is a geothermal spa with milky blue waters located in a lava field near Grindavik. It's a great area for rest and relaxation.

The Golden Circle is a popular tourist circuit that contains three major attractions: Thingvellir National Park, where you may walk between the tectonic plates; Gullfoss, one of Iceland's most renowned waterfalls; and the Geysir geothermal region, which is home to the Strokkur geyser.

Seljalandsfoss: This beautiful waterfall is situated on Iceland's South Coast. What distinguishes it is the ability to stroll behind the flowing water, creating a spectacular experience.

Jökulsárlón Glacier Lagoon: Located in southeastern Iceland, Jökulsárlón is a stunning glacial lake with floating icebergs. You may go on a boat excursion or just enjoy the beautiful views.

Reynisfjara Black Sand Beach: This black sand beach near the settlement of Vk is notable for its spectacular basalt columns and fierce surf. It's an excellent spot for a beautiful stroll and to take in the raw beauty of Iceland's shoreline.

Landmannalaugar: famed for its colorful rhyolite mountains, hot springs, and hiking routes, this strange location in Iceland's Highlands is famed for its unearthly landscape. It's a nature lover's and outdoor enthusiast's dream.

Dettifoss: The most powerful waterfall in Europe, Dettifoss is situated in Vatnajökull National Park. Its tremendous fall, along with the surrounding rough environment, creates an enthralling picture.

Skaftafell Nature Reserve: Skaftafell, which is part of Vatnajökull National Park, has a number of hiking paths that lead to spectacular glaciers, waterfalls, and panoramic overlooks. Hikers and wildlife photographers will love it.

Snaefellsjökull National Park: This national park, located on the Snaefellsnes Peninsula, is home to the famed Snfellsjökull volcano. The region is famous for its varied scenery, which include lava fields, moss-covered slopes, and stunning cliffs.

Reykjavik: With its bustling art scene, unusual architecture, and beautiful streets, Iceland's capital city is worth seeing. Visit the majestic Hallgrimskirkja church, the Harpa music center, and the vibrant cafés and eateries.

These are just a handful of the numerous attractions available in Iceland. The country's natural splendor and distinct landscapes make it a dream destination for adventurers and those seeking remarkable experiences.

Who Should Visit Iceland?

Iceland is a fascinating destination with a unique combination of natural beauties, outdoor excursions, and cultural encounters. It is a site that will appeal to a broad spectrum of visitors. Here are some examples of persons who would appreciate visiting Iceland:

Solo Travelers : Iceland is regarded as a safe and pleasant place for single visitors. It's a perfect spot for a solo journey, thanks to its well-established tourist infrastructure and welcoming inhabitants. Whether you're searching for solitude in nature or to meet other travelers at hostels and social events, Iceland is a terrific place for solo exploration.

Family Vacation: Iceland is a family-friendly location offering a variety of activities and attractions for visitors of all ages. Children will love exploring lava tunnels, visiting petting zoos, riding Icelandic horses, and swimming in geothermal pools. Many tour operators and lodgings cater exclusively to families, ensuring that everyone has a memorable and delightful time.

Nature enthusiasts: Nature lovers will enjoy Iceland's stunning landscapes, which include volcanoes, glaciers, waterfalls, geothermal zones, and black sand beaches. Nature enthusiasts will enjoy visiting the Golden Circle, Ring Road, Jökulsárlón Glacier Lagoon, Landmannalaugar, and Snaefellsnes Peninsula.

Adventure seekers: Iceland has a plethora of outdoor activities for adrenaline seekers. Hiking, glacier climbing, ice cave exploration, snorkeling or diving in the Silfra fissure, horseback riding, whale viewing, and even skiing in the winter months are all options.

Photography enthusiasts: Photographers will love Iceland because of its breathtaking natural beauty and unusual lighting conditions. There are numerous options for amazing images, from catching the Northern Lights to photographing renowned scenery.

History and culture buffs: Iceland has a rich cultural legacy and a fascinating past for history and culture aficionados. The capital city, Reykjavik, is home to museums, art galleries, and historical buildings such as the Hallgrimskirkja cathedral and the National Museum of Iceland. In addition, the nation boasts a thriving music industry and holds several festivals throughout the year.

Wildlife enthusiasts: Wildlife aficionados will enjoy seeing puffins, seals, reindeer, and numerous bird species in Iceland. Visitors may witness these species in their native habitats by taking wildlife excursions or visiting nature reserves.

Outdoor enthusiasts: Due to its difficult terrain and pure natural surroundings, Iceland is a fantastic location for outdoor activities. Hiking, rock climbing, mountain biking, kayaking, and fishing are popular activities among adventurous vacationers. These activities are set against a spectacular background of stunning surroundings.

Food and culinary explorers: Iceland's culinary sector is expanding, with an emphasis on fresh, locally produced foods. Traditional Icelandic cuisine such as lamb, fish, skyr (a kind of yogurt), and unusual specialties such as pickled shark and Icelandic moss are available to visitors. Exploring

Reykjavik's restaurants and local food markets may give a delectable introduction to the country's cuisine.

In conclusion, Iceland is a fascinating and intriguing place that appeals to a broad spectrum of visitors. Iceland's breathtaking landscapes, cultural legacy, and friendly hospitality make it a must-visit whether you're an outdoor enthusiast, history buff, nature lover, or just searching for a unique experience.

Best Adventure Activities

Iceland is famous for its stunning scenery and one-of-a-kind outdoor adventures. Here are some of the top adventurous activities in Iceland for tourists:

Glacier Hiking: Crampon up and join a guided trek on glaciers like Sólheimajökull or Vatnajökull to explore Iceland's beautiful glaciers. You'll see spectacular ice formations as well as breathtaking panoramic vistas.

Ice Cave Exploration: Ice caverns emerge inside glaciers throughout the winter months, creating an unearthly experience. Explore these magnificent ice sculptures with a guided tour and take great images.

Silfra is a fissure in Thingvellir National Park that offers crystal-clear water clarity for snorkeling and diving. Take a guided snorkeling or diving excursion to see the fascinating underwater environment and the once-in-a-lifetime experience of swimming between tectonic plates.

Whale viewing: Iceland is one of Europe's top destinations for whale viewing. Join a boat excursion from Reykjavik, Hsavk, or other coastal towns to see whales like humpbacks, orcas, and minke whales.

ATV/Quad Biking: Ride an ATV or quad bike across Iceland's rocky landscape. Off-road trips through lava fields, black sand beaches, and hilly vistas are available.

Riding Icelandic horses are noted for their unusual stride and amiable disposition. Explore Iceland's breathtaking scenery on horseback, including lava fields, pastures, and picturesque pathways.

Volcano Tours: Iceland's volcanic activity provides an opportunity to see volcanic landscapes up close. Take a guided excursion to an active or dormant volcano, such as

Fimmvöruháls or the Askja Caldera, and experience nature's raw force.

Super Jeep Tours: Take a super jeep trip to see Iceland's isolated and rough landscapes. These adapted 4x4 vehicles can transport you to locations that ordinary automobiles cannot, such as the Highlands, where you will see breathtaking landscapes and natural treasures.

River Rafting: Rafting along Iceland's glacier rivers is a thrilling experience. Join a guided river rafting experience to negotiate rapids and take in the beauty along the way.

Paragliding: Fly over Iceland's breathtaking landscapes while paragliding. Soar over mountains, waterfalls, and volcanic regions on a tandem flight with an expert instructor.

To protect your safety and the preservation of Iceland's beautiful ecosystem, hire trustworthy tour companies and follow their rules.

Festivals & Events that Shouldn't Be Missed

Throughout the year, Iceland is recognized for its colorful festivals and events. Here are some of Iceland's must-see festivals, events, and carnival seasons:

Reykjavik Winter Lights Festival: This festival, held in February, celebrates the winter season with a variety of events such as magnificent light displays, concerts, cultural performances, and outdoor activities.

Secret Solstice event: Held in Reykjavik around the summer solstice in June, this music event comprises both local and international performers playing in exotic locales such as glaciers and lava caverns.

Icelandic National Day: This holiday, observed on June 17th, commemorates Iceland's independence from Denmark. Parades, live music, traditional dances, and outdoor activities are among the festivities held in towns and cities around the nation.

Reykjavik Arts Festival: Held in May and June, this annual arts festival features a diverse spectrum of performances, exhibits, and installations by local and international artists. It includes a variety of art disciplines such as music, theater, dance, and visual arts.

jóhát (The National celebration): This celebration, held in late July in the Westman Islands, is one of Iceland's major outdoor events. There will be live music, bonfires, fireworks, and a fun camping environment. It's a popular gathering for both residents and tourists.

Iceland Airwaves: Iceland Airwaves, the country's main music event, takes place in November in Reykjavik. It features a wide roster of Icelandic and international musicians at a variety of venues across the city.

Sónar Reykjavík: This electronic music event takes place in February and draws both established and new electronic music performers. It provides a one-of-a-kind and intimate setting for music enthusiasts.

Culture Night (Menningarnótt): Every August, Reykjavik comes alive with art exhibits, live concerts, food booths, and cultural events for people of all ages.

Winter Festivals: around the winter months, many winter festivals are hosted around Iceland, including activities like ice skating, snowboarding, snowmobiling, and ice fishing. The Akureyri Winter Festival and the Skammdegi Festival in Siglufjörur are two famous events.

New Year's Eve: Icelanders ring in the New Year with spectacular fireworks displays and bonfires in cities and villages around the nation. The fireworks display in Reykjavik is especially well-known, drawing large crowds.

These are only a handful of the many festivals, events, and carnival seasons that occur throughout Iceland. The rich cultural landscape of the nation means that there is always something intriguing going on throughout the year.

Top Tourist Cities to Stay In Iceland

Iceland has a variety of hotel alternatives to meet a variety of tastes and budgets. When picking where to stay in Iceland, keep your vacation plan, chosen activities, and personal tastes in mind. Here are some popular lodging spots to consider:

Reykjavik: As the capital city, Reykjavik has a variety of lodgings, ranging from luxury hotels to budget-friendly hostels. Staying in Reykjavik puts you in close proximity to the city's cultural attractions, restaurants, and nightlife. It's also a good starting point for day visits to surrounding sights like the Golden Circle.

Golden Circle: If you wish to be near Iceland's famed Golden Circle path, stay in the surrounding villages of Selfoss or Hella. This area has a combination of hotels, guesthouses, and farm stays, allowing visitors to enjoy the lovely countryside while visiting major sights like as Geysir, Gullfoss waterfall, and Thingvellir National Park.

South Coast: Iceland's South Coast is noted for its breathtaking scenery, which include waterfalls, black sand beaches, and glaciers. Accommodation choices range from hotels to guesthouses in towns like Vik and Hella, and they serve as good bases for visiting the sights along the South Coast, including as the waterfalls Seljalandsfoss and Skogafoss.

Akureyri is the second-largest city in Iceland, located in northern Iceland. It has a pleasant ambiance and is surrounded by lovely fjords and mountains. Akureyri has a wide range of lodging options, including hotels, guesthouses, and flats. This area is ideal for experiencing northern Iceland's magnificent scenery, such as Lake Myvatn and the Dettifoss waterfall.

Westfjords: If you want to go somewhere secluded and off the main road, try lodging in the Westfjords. This area has spectacular natural splendor, including fjords, cliffs, and animals. Accommodation choices in towns like Isafjordur and Patreksfjordur range from guesthouses to modest cottages.

It's crucial to know that Iceland's tourist business has been significantly expanding in recent years, so plan ahead of time, particularly during the peak vacation season (June to August). Depending on your budget and tastes, you may also explore camping, since Iceland offers a number of well-equipped campgrounds located around the nation.

Chapter Four

Eco-Friendly Hotels & Resorts With Their Prices Rates

Iceland is recognized for its magnificent natural scenery, and the country's dedication to sustainability and environmental protection is nicely complemented by its eco-friendly hotels. These lodgings provide a distinct combination of luxury, relaxation, and social facilities, providing an enjoyable and environmentally conscientious visit.

Iceland's eco-friendly lodgings vary in luxury from quaint cottages secluded in the countryside to contemporary eco-hotels in the heart of the city. To give customers a pleasant and environmentally conscientious experience, these businesses emphasize the use of sustainable materials and energy-efficient technology. Expect comfortable mattresses, well-equipped rooms, and facilities that meet your requirements while reducing environmental effect.

Relaxation is an important part of Iceland's environmentally friendly hotels. Many of them are deliberately placed near natural treasures like hot springs, geothermal spas, or breathtaking hiking routes. Relax in geothermal pools, indulge in spa treatments made with natural and locally produced materials, or just enjoy the peace and quiet of nature. The focus on sustainable techniques extends to various relaxation options, ensuring that your rejuvenation has minimum environmental impact.

Social amenities are essential in Iceland's environmentally friendly housing. Many businesses prioritize public places where customers may socialize, exchange experiences, and build a feeling of community. Common spaces are often designed with eco-friendly components such as salvaged wood, renewable energy sources, and locally made artwork. Furthermore, educational events such as seminars on sustainable living or guided excursions to discover Iceland's eco-friendly efforts are routinely organized by these hotels.

Overall, Iceland's eco-friendly lodgings provide a balanced combination of luxury, relaxation, and social facilities, all while adhering to the country's environmental commitment. By staying at these places, you may have a wonderful visit in Iceland while reducing your carbon impact and supporting sustainable tourism practices.

Budget Friendly Tourist Hotels & Resorts

Iceland has a variety of budget-friendly hotels and resorts for visitors. Here are a few alternatives, along with their estimated costs:

Hlemmur Square (Reykjavik): Hlemmur Square is a low-cost hotel in the center of Reykjavik. It has both private rooms and dorm-style accommodations. Prices per night start at $80 USD.

Fosshótel Reykjavík (Reykjavik): The Fosshotel Reykjavik is a contemporary hotel situated in downtown Reykjavik. It has pleasant accommodations as well as facilities. Prices per night start at $100 USD.

Hotel Cabin (Reykjavik): Hotel Cabin is a low-cost hotel in the city center. It provides minimal conveniences in modest and tidy rooms. Prices per night start at $70 USD.

Hótel rk (Hveragerdi): Hótel rk is a low-cost hotel in the village of Hveragerdi, which is noted for its hot springs. It has spacious rooms, a swimming pool, and hot tubs. Prices per night start at $90 USD.

Hotel Geysir (Geysir): Hotel Geysir is located in the Geysir geothermal area in the famed Golden Circle region. It provides inexpensive accommodations with breathtaking views. The nightly rate starts at $120 USD.

Hótel Laxnes (Mosfellsbaer): Hótel Laxnes is a pleasant hotel in Mosfellsbær, only a short drive from Reykjavik. It has pleasant accommodations and a welcoming environment. Prices per night start at $90 USD.

Luxury Tourist Hotels and Resorts

Iceland has a number of upscale hotels and resorts that appeal to discriminating travelers. Here are a few noteworthy alternatives, along with their projected costs:

The Retreat at Blue Lagoon: The Retreat at Blue Lagoon, located amid the spectacular lava landscapes of Grindavik, provides a special experience with its own geothermal spa and breathtaking views. A one-night stay at this premium resort costs about $1,000.

Hotel Rangá: Hotel Rangá, located in the countryside near Hella, is known for its secluded position and great stargazing prospects. This hotel offers a unique combination of comfort and natural beauty with its warm and beautiful rooms. A one-night stay at Hotel Rangá normally costs between $500 and $1,000.

Ion Adventure Hotel: Ion Adventure Hotel provides a modern design influenced by Icelandic nature, set against the stunning backdrop of Mount Hengill. Its proximity to Thingvellir National Park makes it an ideal starting point for exploring the Golden Circle. A one-night stay at Ion Adventure Hotel typically costs roughly $400.

The Northern Light Inn: The Northern Light Inn, located near the Blue Lagoon, offers a quiet and personal ambiance. The rustic appeal of the hotel, as well as its closeness to spectacular natural features, make it a wonderful option for tourists. A one-night stay at The Northern Light Inn normally costs between $200 and $400.

Hotel Borg: Hotel Borg, located in the center of Reykjavik, blends Art Deco beauty with contemporary facilities. Its central position provides convenient access to the city's major attractions, shopping, and restaurants. A one-night stay at Hotel Borg typically costs roughly $300.

Please keep in mind that these are estimates and may vary based on the season, availability, and individual room types. It is always best to check with hotels directly or via online booking platforms for the most up-to-date pricing and availability information.

Vacation Rentals and Apartments

Visitors visiting Iceland may pick from a wide range of apartments and holiday rentals. The cost of these lodgings varies based on location, size, facilities, and the time of year you want to visit. Keep in mind that rates are subject to change, so for the most up-to-date information, always check with particular rental listings or websites. Following are some general guidelines:

Reykjavik: As the capital city, Reykjavik offers a diverse choice of apartment rentals. A one-bedroom apartment in the city center may cost $150 to $300 a night, while a bigger two-bedroom apartment may cost $250 to $500 per night. Prices are somewhat cheaper outside of the city center.

Self-catering cottages: For a more private experience, consider renting a cottage in Iceland's countryside. These often have kitchens and are perfect for self-catering. The cost of a cottage varies based on its location and size. A cottage rental will typically cost between $150 and $400 per night.

Vacation rentals and guesthouses: There are many vacation rentals and guest houses available around Iceland. These choices vary from small flats to bigger residences with many bedrooms. Prices might vary widely based on location and degree of luxury. A vacation rental or guesthouse will typically cost between $100 and $300 per night.

Campervans and motorhomes: Renting a campervan or motorhome is another popular way to see Iceland. These combine transportation and lodging into a single package. Prices for campervan rentals vary based on size and time of year, but you can expect to spend between $150 and $400 per night on average.

It's worth mentioning that Iceland is often regarded as an expensive vacation, and lodging rates might be greater than in other nations. Furthermore, rates are often higher during the peak tourist season, which runs from June to August. If your vacation dates are flexible, going during the shoulder seasons (spring or autumn) might result in reduced lodging expenses.

When picking lodgings in Iceland, remember to study and compare various rental alternatives, read reviews, and consider your personal requirements and budget.

Iceland Hostels and Guesthouse

Iceland has a variety of guesthouses and hostels to serve guests of all budgets. The price depends on the location, facilities, and season. Here are some of the most popular guesthouses and hostels in Iceland, along with an estimate of their prices:

Reykjavik Downtown Hostel: This hostel, located in the center of Reykjavik, provides both dormitory-style and private rooms. Prices per night vary from around $25 to $100, depending on the accommodation type and season.

Loft Hostel: Located in the heart of Reykjavik, Loft Hostel offers a stylish and sociable environment. Dorm beds start about $30 per night, while private rooms may range between $80 and $150 per night.

Kex Hostel: Kex Hostel is another popular option in Reykjavik, with a distinctive and vintage-inspired environment. Dorm beds start about $30 per night, while private rooms cost between $90 and $200 per night.

Hlemmur Square: Hlemmur Square is a trendy hostel near Reykjavik's major bus terminal that offers both dormitory beds and private rooms. Dormitory beds start about $35 per night, while private rooms cost between $80 and $150 each night.

Akureyri Backpackers: Akureyri Backpackers is a popular option in the northern Icelandic town of Akureyri. Dorm beds start about $30 per night, while private rooms cost between $90 and $150 per night.

Hostelling International - Skaftafell: Located near Vatnajökull National Park, this hostel provides a convenient base for enjoying Iceland's breathtaking natural beauty. Dormitory beds start about $30 per night, while private rooms vary between $80 and $150 per night.

Guesthouse Borgartun: Located in Reykjavik, Guesthouse Borgartun offers inexpensive lodging with shared amenities. A double room starts at roughly $70 per night.

Please keep in mind that these are estimations and may vary depending on variables such as season, availability, and any extra services or facilities provided by each institution. It's usually a good idea to verify current pricing and availability with the guesthouse or hostel where you want to stay.

Iceland Tourist Camp Venues

Here is some basic information regarding camping places and rates in Iceland, but please keep in mind that specifics may vary based on the time of year, availability, and the sort of camping experience you want.

Campsites: Iceland offers a large number of campsites scattered around the nation, ranging from primitive sites with few amenities to more developed campgrounds with amenities such as showers, cooking areas, and power. Among the most popular campsites are:

Reykjavik: The city's Reykjavik Campsite is a popular alternative for people looking to explore the capital and its surroundings.

The famed Golden Circle path includes various campsites, including Selfoss and Laugarvatn. These areas are convenient for visiting sights such as Geysir, Gullfoss, and Thingvellir National Park.

South Coast: Campgrounds on the South Coast include Skógafoss, Vk, and Kirkjubaejarklaustur. These locations are ideal for visiting sights like Seljalandsfoss, Skógafoss, and Reynisfjara beach.

North Iceland: Campgrounds may be found in communities such as Akureyri, Hsavk, and Myvatn in northern Iceland. These places are noted for their beautiful scenery and accessibility to attractions like Dettifoss, Lake Myvatn, and whale viewing in Husk.

Costs: The cost of camping in Iceland varies according to the campsite and the amenities offered. A modest campsite with inadequate amenities will typically cost between 1,500 and 2,500 ISK per person per night. More upscale campgrounds may charge between 2,500 and 4,500 ISK per person per night. Discounts are also available at several campsites for children and bigger parties.

Furthermore, some campsites demand the purchase of a camping card, which provides you access to a network of participating campgrounds around the nation for a specified length of time. The camping card costs roughly 15,000 to 18,000 ISK and is usable for a certain period of time, often 28 to 30 days.

Wild camping (camping outside licensed campsites) is permitted in Iceland, although specific standards must be observed to limit environmental harm and protect private property.

Chapter Five

Historical Monuments And Icelandic Heritage

In the middle of Iceland's stunning landscapes, a country of fire and ice, lies a legacy that hints of ancient times. Its historical monuments serve as quiet testimony to a nation's tenacity and spirit, retaining echoes of a rich history. Iceland's history is a tapestry woven with sagas of ferocious Vikings, sagas that merge with nature's untamed powers to create a compelling tale. Every step in this area of breathtaking beauty is a journey to a nation's origins, where the present meets the past and history becomes a live, breathing presence.

Here are some of Iceland's most noteworthy heritage sites and historical monuments:

Thingvellir National Park: Thingvellir, located near Reykjavik, is a UNESCO World Heritage site with tremendous historical and cultural significance for Iceland. It was the location of the Althing, one of the world's oldest operating legislatures, which was founded in 930 AD. Thingvellir is also located on the Mid-Atlantic Ridge, which connects the Eurasian and North American tectonic plates, making it a geologically important position.

Reykholt: During the 13th century, this historic place in western Iceland was the residence of the famed Icelandic poet and historian Snorri Sturluson. Snorri Sturluson's works, such as the Prose Edda and Heimskringla, were critical in preserving Norse mythology and sagas.

Skálholt: Skálholt was the ecclesiastical and educational hub of Iceland from the 11th through the 18th century. It was the bishops' seat and a significant center for academic and cultural activity.

Akureyrarkirkja: This historic church is a notable landmark in Akureyri, Iceland's second-largest city. It was designed by Gujón Samuelsson and finished in 1940, and it has a distinct architectural style influenced by Icelandic landscape and mythology.

Settlement Exhibition, Reykjavik: This museum in Reykjavik provides information on the Viking Age and Iceland's settlement. It is centered on the ruins of a

Viking-era longhouse uncovered during archaeological digs, and it houses relics and interactive exhibitions.

The Sun Voyager (Sólfar): This renowned sculpture by Jón Gunnar , located on the Reykjavik waterfront, depicts a Viking ship, signifying the spirit of exploration and adventure. It has become an icon of Reykjavik and is a major tourist attraction.

Skógafoss: While not a typical historical monument, Skógafoss is a spectacular waterfall situated along Iceland's southern shore. It is often connected with mythology and folklore, which adds to its cultural importance.

These are only a few examples of Iceland's history and historical monuments. Visitors may learn about Iceland's unique history, customs, and cultural heritage by visiting these locations.

Contemporary Art Galleries And Museums

Iceland has a thriving contemporary art culture, with galleries and institutions displaying the work of both

Icelandic and foreign artists. Here are some of Iceland's most renowned modern art galleries and museums:

Reykjavik Art Museum (RAM): RAM is Iceland's biggest visual art institution, with three locations: Hafnarhus, Kjarvalsstair, and . Various contemporary art exhibits are held in the museum, showcasing both Icelandic and foreign artists.

Listasafn Einars Jónssonar: This museum in Reykjavik is devoted to the works of Icelandic artist Einar Jónsson. It has a collection of his sculptures and provides visitors with an insight into his creative career.

Hverfisgaller: Hverfisgaller is a contemporary art gallery in Reykjavik's city center that exhibits works by rising Icelandic artists. Experimentation and innovation are often featured at the gallery.

i8 Gallery: Located in Reykjavik, i8 Gallery is known for its emphasis on contemporary art and recognized artists. It exhibits a wide variety of works, such as paintings, sculptures, installations, and video art.

Kling & Bang Gallery: Kling & Bang is an artist-run gallery in Reykjavik's city center that showcases contemporary art by Icelandic and international artists. The gallery's mission is to encourage experimental and conceptual art.

Hafnarborg - The Hafnarfjörur Centre of Culture and Fine Art: Hafnarborg is a modern art museum and cultural institution located near Reykjavik. It features changing exhibits of modern art, including pieces by Icelandic artists.

The Living Art Museum (Nló) is a non-profit artist-run organization in Reykjavik that was founded in 1978. It promotes experimental and multidisciplinary works while promoting current art practices.

Skaftfell - Center for Visual Art: Skaftfell is an interdisciplinary center for visual art located in Seyisfjörur, a tiny village in eastern Iceland. It is a nexus for artists, residents, and foreign tourists, and it holds exhibits, residencies, and events.

These are only a handful of the modern art galleries and museums available in Iceland. Because the country's art landscape is always changing, it's worth keeping an eye out for new and temporary exhibits throughout your stay.

National Parks And Reserve

Iceland features a number of national parks and reserves that highlight the country's distinctive geology, fauna, and natural beauty. Here are some of Iceland's most notable national parks and reserves:

1: Vatnajökull National Park, located in southern Iceland, is Europe's biggest national park, comprising an area of about 14,141 square kilometers (5,460 square miles). It has the biggest glacier in Europe, Vatnajökull, as well as several volcanoes, glacial rivers, and different habitats.

2: Pingvellir National Park: National Park is located approximately 40 kilometers (25 miles) east of Reykjavik and is rich in historical and geological importance. It is the location of the Icelandic Parliament, Alingi, which was created in 930 AD, making it one of the world's oldest legislative venues. The park also includes the stunning Almannagjá Gorge and the location where the North American and Eurasian tectonic plates collide.

69

3: Snaefellsjökull National Park: Snfellsjökull National Park is located on the Snaefellsnes Peninsula in western Iceland and is home to the beautiful Snfellsjökull glacier-capped volcano. The park's landforms are diversified, including lava fields, coastal cliffs, and black sand beaches. It served as the inspiration for Jules Verne's classic book "Journey to the Center of the Earth."

4: Jökulsárgljúfur National Park: Located in northern Iceland, Jökulsárgljfur National Park is known for its stunning rock formations, roaring waterfalls, and magnificent canyons. The park's most popular features are Dettifoss, Europe's most powerful waterfall, and a horseshoe-shaped canyon.

5: The Snaefellsnes Peninsula is a natural reserve recognized for its great beauty, although it is not an official national park. It has a diverse terrain that includes glaciers, volcanic peaks, lava fields, and coastal cliffs. This region's features include the renowned Kirkjufell peak and the picturesque fishing towns of Arnarstapi and Hellnar.

These are only a few examples of Iceland's national parks and reserves. Each of these regions offers hiking, animal viewing, and exploration of Iceland's distinctive geological characteristics. It's worth mentioning that Iceland puts a high value on maintaining its natural heritage, and tourists are urged to practice responsible tourism and adhere to park laws in order to safeguard these fragile ecosystems.

Gardens and Romantic Couples Packs

Couples may enjoy a range of romantic activities in Iceland, from beautiful scenery to quaint gardens.

Reykjavik Botanical Gardens: Located in Reykjavik's capital city, the Botanical Gardens provide a tranquil location for couples to wander hand in hand. The gardens include a wide range of plants, including both local Icelandic species and foreign vegetation. The tranquil setting makes it perfect for a romantic picnic or a leisurely stroll.

Akureyri Botanical Garden: Located in the northern Iceland town of Akureyri, the Akureyri Botanical Garden is recognized for its wide array of plants, flowers, and trees. The garden's well-kept walks and colorful displays create a romantic environment, providing a great location for couples to explore and enjoy each other's company.

Stóra-ásgeirsá (Garden of Eden): This private garden is situated in southern Iceland, near the town of Hveragerdi. It has a lovely collection of flowers, waterfalls, and a diversity of vegetation. The Garden of Eden provides a romantic and peaceful atmosphere for couples wishing to spend quality time together while being surrounded by nature's magnificence.

The Golden Circle: The Golden Circle, one of Iceland's most famous tourist itineraries, allows couples to see various natural beauties together. This path passes through Þingvellir National Park, the Geysir Geothermal Area, and the Gullfoss waterfall. The Golden Circle's spectacular vistas and awe-inspiring views create a romantic background for memorable encounters.

The Blue Lagoon: While not technically a garden, the Blue Lagoon is a well-known geothermal bath on a lava field on the Reykjanes Peninsula. Couples may unwind in the warm, mineral-rich waters while taking in the breathtaking natural landscape. The tranquil setting and soothing waves make it a favorite location for couples looking for a romantic and refreshing encounter.

When arranging a romantic holiday to Iceland, consider visiting the country's scenic landscapes, such as Vik's black sand beaches, the ice caves in Vatnajökull National Park, or the breathtaking waterfalls Seljalandsfoss and Skógafoss. The natural beauty of Iceland offers various possibilities for couples to interact and make unforgettable memories together.

Zoos And Educational Museums

Iceland is famous for its breathtaking natural beauty, which includes unusual fauna and beautiful landscapes.

Nonetheless, Iceland has a few attractions and educational institutions where visitors may learn about the country's natural history and fauna. Here are a few examples:

1: The Icelandic Museum of Natural History (Náttúrufræðistofnun íslands): This museum, located in Reykjavik, Iceland's capital city, concentrates on the natural history of Iceland and its surrounding seas. It includes displays on geology, botany, zoology, and paleontology, highlighting the country's rich flora and wildlife. The museum's holdings comprise a wide range of specimens and artifacts that serve as great instructional tools.

2: The Whales of Iceland Museum is located in Reykjavik and is devoted to displaying the spectacular marine creatures present in Iceland's seas. It provides visitors with an immersive experience with interactive exhibitions and life-sized whale sculptures. The museum also gives educational material on whale conservation and the significance of maintaining these magnificent species.

3: The Sea Ice Exhibition: This exhibition, located in Höfn, a town in southeastern Iceland, focuses on the Arctic area and the influence of climate change on sea ice. It investigates the connection between sea ice, marine life, and global climate systems. The exhibition includes educational exhibits and multimedia presentations to raise awareness about the Arctic ecosystem's vulnerability.

4: The Husavik Whale Museum: Located in Husk, renowned as the "Whale Watching Capital of Europe," this museum presents in-depth information on whales and their cultural importance in Iceland. Exhibits include whale anatomy, behavior, and conservation initiatives. The museum also provides educational events and guided tours to help visitors better comprehend these wonderful animals.

5: The Sólheimar Ecovillage is a sustainable community situated in southern Iceland that is not exactly a zoo or museum. It focuses on organic agriculture, renewable energy, and environmentally friendly lifestyle. Various animal-related activities, such as animal-assisted therapy programs and horse therapy, are included into the community. Visitors may learn about sustainable methods and get a fresh take on environmental education.

These sites provide fascinating insights into Iceland's natural heritage and the significance of conservation. While Iceland lacks typical zoos, these museums and educational experiences allow visitors to learn about the country's rich wildlife and develop an understanding for its fragile ecosystems.

Chapter Six

Iceland's Nightlife At A Glance

Step into the enchanted world of Iceland's nightlife, where the Northern Lights dazzle the sky and music fills the air. This kingdom of fire and ice inspires a thirst for celebration, where residents and tourists join beneath the cover of night to create memories that gleam with a touch of enchantment, from fashionable bars to quaint pubs. The streets of Reykjavik, Iceland's capital city, come alive with laughing, stories, and glass clinking, beckoning you to immerse yourself in a unique nighttime journey. The nightlife in Iceland is a symphony of warmth, friendship, and memorable experiences set to the pulse of an incredible spirit.

A Guide To Iceland Active Bars and Nightclubs

Iceland has a thriving nightlife culture with a wide range of busy pubs and nightclubs to suit all preferences. Here is a list of several popular active establishments in Reykjavik, Iceland's capital city:

Kiki Queer Bar: Kiki Queer Bar, located in downtown Reykjavik, is a lively and welcoming establishment noted for its bright atmosphere and frenetic dance floor. Drag performances, themed parties, and a mix of local and foreign DJs playing energetic music are all held at the bar.

Pablo Discobar: Pablo Discobar is a retro-themed nightclub that draws a youthful and dynamic population. It is inspired by the '80s and '90s. The dance floor is constantly busy, and the DJs play a variety of disco, pop, and electronic music. There are also neon lights, arcade games, and a dancing cage at the venue.

Austur: Austur is a prominent nightclub in Reykjavik noted for its vibrant ambience and beautiful décor. Austur provides a range of music genres, including hip-hop, house, and R&B, with various dance floors and bars distributed over different levels.

Paloma is a multi-purpose facility that accommodates concerts, DJ sets, and themed events. The main floor of the club is ideal for dancing, while the upper level has a more calm lounge area. Paloma includes a diverse range of musical genres, ranging from indie and alternative to electronic and techno.

Hrra is a trendy and alternative music venue with a dynamic vibe. The pub often presents live concerts by local and international indie bands. Aside from concerts, Hrra morphs into a dance club with DJs performing alternative and rock music.

Harlem: Harlem is well-known for its soul, funk, and jazz music, and it is a popular location for live concerts and dancing. The facility has a throwback atmosphere, and the dance floor fills up as the night goes on. Harlem also has a comfortable bar where you may have a drink while listening to live music.

Priki: Priki, one of Reykjavik's oldest pubs, has become a city institution. It is a casual café during the day, but at night it turns into a crowded bar with a colorful ambiance. Priki presents live music events, DJ performances, and themed evenings that include a wide variety of music genres.

Remember that the nightlife scene in Reykjavik might change, so check the schedules and activities of these businesses ahead of time. Additionally, when enjoying Iceland's bustling pubs and nightclubs, be mindful of local legislation and be courteous of the venue's rules as well as other clients.

How to Locate Live Music Venues and Jazz Clubs

Follow these procedures to discover live music venues and jazz bars in Iceland:

1; Begin by making an internet search using a search engine such as Google or Bing. To discover relevant results, use keywords like "live music venues Iceland" or "jazz bars in Iceland." Investigate the websites and listings that come up in the search results.

2: Check out social media networks such as Facebook, Instagram, and Twitter. Many music venues and pubs have their own social media profiles where they promote upcoming acts and events. Follow the sites of prominent Icelandic music venues and jazz bars to remain up to date on their schedules.

3; Local Event Listings: Look for local event listings websites that cover events in Iceland, both general and music-specific. Tix.is and Eventful, for example, often advertise live music performances, including jazz gigs. Look for listings in categories like "Music" or "Concerts" to locate relevant listings.

4: Ask Locals or Expats: Use internet forums, social media groups, or travel communities to connect with Icelandic residents or expats. They may provide personal suggestions and insights into the area's greatest live music venues and jazz pubs.

5: Visit Tourist Information Centers: Once in Iceland, go to the closest tourist information center. They generally include brochures, maps, and experienced personnel who can tell you about local live music venues and jazz pubs.

6: Explore Reykjavik's Music culture: Reykjavik, Iceland's capital city, has a thriving music culture with various clubs and pubs hosting live music performances. Take a walk across downtown Reykjavik, looking for clubs and pubs that have posters or banners promoting live music events.

7: Attend Music Festivals: Iceland is well-known for its music festivals, which often offer a wide variety of genres, including jazz. Keep an eye out for forthcoming music festivals like the Reykjavik Jazz Festival and other events that include live music performances.

Before attending a certain venue or jazz bar, check the timetables and confirm event information, since they may have variable opening hours and event schedules.

Jazz And live Music Venues

Iceland has a thriving music culture, and although it is not recognized for its jazz, there are various locations where you can hear live music, including jazz concerts. Here are some of Iceland's most popular live music venues:

Harpa Concert Hall (Reykjavik): Harpa is one of Iceland's most prominent music venues, holding a range of concerts and events, including jazz performances, throughout the year. It has a variety of performance areas and is well-known for its superb acoustics.

Dillon Whiskey tavern (Reykjavik): Dillon is a pleasant tavern with live music, including jazz, on a regular basis. It has a laid-back vibe and is a favorite hangout for both locals and visitors wishing to listen to live music.

Kex Hostel (Reykjavik): Kex is more than just a hostel; it's also a popular meeting spot for music fans. It holds regular concerts that often include jazz performers. The facility has a distinct industrial-chic character and is well-known for its trendy ambience.

Bryggjan Brugghus (Reykjavik): This microbrewery and restaurant provides live music events, including jazz performances, on occasion. It attracts both residents and tourists due to its wide assortment of specialty brews and pleasant atmosphere.

Hressingarskálinn (Reykjavik): Hressingarskálinn is a well-known downtown Reykjavik pub that often hosts live music, notably jazz bands. It features a relaxed and energetic environment, making it ideal for unwinding and listening to live music.

Tónleikar Ksi Háteigskirkja (Hafnarfjörður): This concert hall, located just outside of Reykjavik, often holds diverse music acts, including jazz concerts. It is well-known for its great sound quality and cozy atmosphere.

Cafe Rosenberg (Reykjavik): Cafe Rosenberg is a nice cafe and bar with live jazz concerts on a regular basis. It offers a casual environment and is a favorite hangout for jazz fans in Reykjavik.

These are only a handful of the places in Iceland where you may listen to live music, including jazz. However, since the music industry changes over time, it's always a good idea to check their calendars or websites for forthcoming events and performances.

Tips for A Memorable Night in Iceland

If you want to make the most of your night in Iceland, here are some suggestions:

Iceland is well-known for its spectacular displays of the Northern Lights (Aurora Borealis). Check the weather and go somewhere with little light pollution for the greatest possibility of seeing this natural event. Consider taking a guided tour to benefit from experienced expertise and support.

1: Relax in the Blue Lagoon: Take a soak in the Blue Lagoon's geothermal waters. This renowned spa is recognized for its milky blue waters that are rich in minerals and provide a one-of-a-kind and refreshing experience. Enjoy the warm sea while surrounded by Iceland's spectacular environment.

2: Explore the night time in Reykjavik: Reykjavik has a thriving nighttime culture with a variety of pubs, clubs, and live music venues. Explore the local culture with music, dancing, and beverages on Laugavegur Street, the major retail and entertainment zone. Weekends are very active.

3: Try Icelandic food: Make a memorable supper by indulging in Icelandic food. Traditional foods to try include lamb stew, smoked salmon, and skyr (a creamy dairy product). For a genuine experience, look for local eateries that use fresh, locally produced products.

4: Take a Midnight Sun Adventure: If you visit Iceland during the summer, you may see the Midnight Sun phenomena. Take a trek, a road trip, or a guided tour to see how the sun never actually sets beyond the horizon. It produces a one-of-a-kind and strange environment.

5: Visit Waterfalls at Sunset: Iceland is famous for its magnificent waterfalls. Plan a visit to a prominent waterfall, such as Seljalandsfoss or Skógafoss, around sunset. The golden hour illumination adds a wonderful touch to the event, making it unforgettable and gorgeous.

6: Go Whale viewing: Iceland is one of Europe's top sites for whale viewing. Take a whale watching excursion from Reykjavik or another coastal town to see spectacular species like humpback whales, orcas, and dolphins. It's an amazing experience on the seas of Iceland.

7: Consider spending the night camping beneath the stars in one of Iceland's numerous campgrounds. The country's distinctive landscapes provide for a wonderful background for stargazing. Check the weather forecast and prepare proper camping gear.

8: Experience a Midnight Concert: During the summer, keep an eye out for special events or performances. Some places provide midnight concerts where you may listen to live music while basking in the Midnight Sun. It's a genuinely one-of-a-kind and unforgettable experience.

9: Record the memories: Don't forget to bring your camera or smartphone to record the breathtaking scenery, one-of-a-kind experiences, and memorable memories.

Iceland has many gorgeous sites, and you'll want to save those memories.

Always check the weather and road conditions, plan ahead, and be ready for the unexpected. Iceland is a country full of natural beauties, and by following these suggestions, you'll enjoy a fantastic night in this gorgeous place.

Chapter Seven

Iceland Food And Drinks

Exploring Iceland's culinary treasures is like going on a sensory journey, with each taste and drink transporting you to a world of pure bliss. Each meal unfolds a symphony of tastes that stimulate the palette and spark the imagination, from the rich, buttery taste of gravlax to the soft succulence of Icelandic lamb, and the saline freshness of Arctic char to the earthy sweetness of rye bread. Iceland's drinks enhance the dining experience to new heights, leaving an unforgettable impact on your taste buds and a craving for more with each sip of velvety-smooth birch liqueur or the crisp, clear flavors of glacier water. Indulging in Iceland's wonderful food is a memorable experience, a celebration of nature's wealth, and a monument to the country's culinary prowess.

Favorite Food & Cuisines

Icelandic cuisine is noted for its use of fresh, locally obtained foods, with a focus on seafood owing to the country's abundance of coastal waterways. Here are some of Iceland's favorite meals and cuisines:

Seafood: Iceland is well-known for its seafood meals, which include fresh fish including salmon, cod, haddock, and herring. Grilled or pan-fried fish, fish stews, and smoked or cured fish are all traditional Icelandic seafood meals.

Lamb: Due to the animals' free-range grazing in Iceland's natural meadows, Icelandic lamb is known for its taste. Roasted lamb, lamb stew (kjötspa), and hangikjöt (smoked lamb) are all popular lamb meals.

Skyr is a typical Icelandic dairy product having a thicker, creamier consistency than yogurt. It is a popular breakfast or snack choice in Iceland, sometimes served with fruits, granola, or honey.

Pylsur (Hot Dogs): "Pylsur," or Icelandic hot dogs, are a popular street dish. They are often cooked with a lamb, hog, and beef combination and served with a variety of toppings such as ketchup, mustard, remoulade (a mayonnaise-based sauce), crispy fried onions, and raw onions.

Rye Bread: "," or Icelandic rye bread, is a rich, dark, and sweet bread usually made in geothermal furnaces. It is a mainstay in Icelandic cuisine and is often eaten with butter.

Svi (Sheep's Head): While not for everyone, is a traditional Icelandic delicacy made of a singed and boiled sheep's head. During the winter months, it is often served as a celebratory meal.

Plokkfiskur (Icelandic fish stew): Plokkfiskur (Icelandic fish stew) is cooked with flaky white fish (typically cod or haddock), potatoes, onions, and milk or cream. It's usually seasoned with salt, pepper, and, sometimes, other herbs.

Icelandic Pastries: Delicious pastries from Iceland include (twisted fried pastry), vinarterta (layered cake with prune jam), and (deep-fried dough).

These are only a few examples of Icelandic cuisines and meals. Icelandic cuisine combines traditional Nordic tastes with contemporary culinary influences, making it a must-try for foodies visiting the country.

Favorite Drinks in Iceland

Iceland is well-known for its unusual and refreshing drinks, especially those produced from local ingredients. Here are a handful of Iceland's favorite drinks:

Brennivn: Brennivn is a traditional Icelandic schnapps flavored with caraway seeds and prepared from fermented potato mash. It is known as the "Black Death" because of its reputation as a powerful and potent liquor.

Icelandic Craft Beers: There is a booming craft beer culture in Iceland, with multiple brewers creating a diverse variety of unusual and tasty beers. Olvisholt Brewery, Einstök Beer Company, and Borg Brugghs are three prominent Icelandic artisan brewers.

Dandelion and Burdock Soda: This is a popular traditional Icelandic soda produced from the roots of dandelion and burdock. It has a characteristic herbal and somewhat sweet flavor, and many Icelanders regard it as a sentimental beverage.

Icelandic Herbal Teas: Iceland is well-known for its diverse range of wild plants, many of which are used to produce herbal teas. Icelandic moss tea, angelica tea, and arctic thyme tea are all popular herbal beverages in Iceland.

Glacier Water: Iceland is famous for its mineral-rich glacier water. Many Icelanders like drinking pure glacier water, which they regard to be among the best-tasting and purest accessible.

These are just a handful of Iceland's favorite beverages. The nation provides a vast range of refreshing and one-of-a-kind drinks that represent its culture and natural resources.

Vegan and Vegetarian Options

For those following a plant-based diet, Iceland, famed for its gorgeous scenery and unusual food, provides a choice of vegetarian and vegan alternatives. While traditional Icelandic cuisine is heavy on fish and meat, there has been a significant increase in knowledge and demand for vegetarian and vegan choices. Here are some possibilities to consider:

Eateries in Reykjavik: The capital city of Iceland, Reykjavik, features a number of eateries that cater to vegetarian and vegan diets. Gló, Kaffi Vinyl, and Veganaes are a few examples. Salads, soups, burgers, and vegan-friendly adaptations of classic Icelandic cuisine are available at these restaurants.

Vegan/Vegetarian-Friendly Grocery shops: Grocery shops in Iceland provide a range of vegetarian and vegan items. Plant-based alternatives are available at major supermarkets such as Bonus, Kronan, and Hagkaup, and include plant-based milks, tofu, tempeh, vegan cheeses, and a broad variety of fruits and vegetables.

Veggie-Friendly lodgings: Some Icelandic lodgings provide vegetarian and vegan choices to its visitors. You may enquire about their menu and dietary alternatives before making a reservation to guarantee they can meet your requirements. It's also a good idea to let them know ahead of time about your dietary preferences.

Vegetarian & Vegan Tours: If you want to see Iceland's natural beauty while eating vegetarian or vegan food, consider taking a vegetarian or vegan tour. These excursions are particularly tailored to plant-based diets and provide a one-of-a-kind gastronomic experience.

Traditional Icelandic meals: While traditional Icelandic cuisine is concentrated on meat and fish, vegetarian or vegan versions of several meals are available. "Rgbrau," for example, is a classic Icelandic rye bread that is normally vegan, while "Spa" is a vegetable soup that may be made without the use of animal ingredients.

It's worth mentioning that, although the availability of vegetarian and vegan foods has increased, it varies based on place and season. It's usually a good idea to check ahead of time with local restaurants and hotels to verify they can accommodate your dietary needs.

Best Cafes & Restaurants in Iceland

Iceland is recognized for its distinct culinary scene, which features a wide range of tasty and locally produced cuisine. Here are a few of the greatest cafés and restaurants in Iceland:

Dill: Dill is Iceland's first Michelin-starred restaurant, located in Reykjavik. It emphasizes the use of local and sustainable resources in order to develop unique meals influenced by traditional Icelandic cuisine.

Grillmarkadurinn (Grill Market): Grillmarkadurinn, located in the center of Reykjavik, provides a contemporary spin on traditional Icelandic meals. The restaurant stresses the use of fresh, local foods and focuses on grilled meats and seafood.

Kopar: Located in Reykjavik's ancient port neighborhood, this restaurant provides a broad cuisine with a combination of Icelandic and foreign tastes. Kopar offers superb fish alternatives and a sleek, modern ambience.

Matur og Drykkur: Located in Reykjavik's Grandi neighborhood, Matur og Drykkur provides a one-of-a-kind dining experience with an emphasis on traditional Icelandic food. Salted cod, lamb, and pickled shark are among the delicacies on the menu that highlight the country's gastronomic tradition.

Slippbarinn: A renowned bar and restaurant noted for its inventive drinks and wonderful cuisine, Slippbarinn is located in Reykjavik's fashionable 101 neighborhood. The menu combines Icelandic and foreign food, and the environment is bright and inviting.

Café Loki: Located near Reykjavik's landmark Hallgrimskirkja cathedral, Café Loki serves traditional Icelandic cuisine in a comfortable environment. The Icelandic rye bread, fermented shark, and numerous fish dishes are popular at the café.

Fridheimar: Fridheimar is a unique restaurant in South Iceland that specializes in cultivating its own tomatoes. It is located along the Golden Circle road. You may have your dinner while surrounded by tomato plants, relishing meals such as tomato soup, spaghetti, and desserts.

Narfeyrarstofa: Located in the town of Stykkishólmur on the Snaefellsnes Peninsula, Narfeyrarstofa is a beautiful seafood restaurant. It serves freshly caught seafood, lobster, and other local specialties on its menu.

Bergsson Maths: Bergsson Mathus is a popular breakfast and brunch place in central Reykjavik. They provide a variety of tasty and healthful alternatives, such as handmade bread, soups, salads, and vegetarian cuisine.

Geysir Bistro: Located in South Iceland's Geysir Geothermal Area, Geysir Bistro is a terrific spot to eat while enjoying the region's natural attractions. Icelandic specialties such as lamb stew, smoked salmon, and baked pastries are on the menu.

These are just a handful of the many amazing cafés and restaurants available in Iceland. Iceland has a lot to offer food enthusiasts, whether they want traditional Icelandic cuisine or foreign dishes with a local touch.

Icelandic Dining Etiquette

Icelandic eating etiquette is usually casual and laid back, although there are certain cultural traditions to bear in mind while dining in the nation. Here are a few crucial considerations to keep in mind:

- Punctuality is essential when invited to someone's house for a dinner or while making a restaurant reservation. It is considered impolite to arrive late without informing the host or restaurant.

- Table manners: It is usual in Iceland to have your hands visible on the table throughout the meal. Resting your elbows on the table is considered disrespectful. Remember to use correct utensils and to prevent slurping or making loud sounds when eating.

- Tipping is not often practiced in Iceland. Because the service fee is often included in the bill, it is unnecessary to give an extra tip. If you believe the service was extraordinary, you may round up the cost or leave a little tip as a token of gratitude.

- Toasting is a prevalent ritual in Icelandic culture, particularly during festive events. When someone makes a toast, establish eye contact with the proposer and raise your glass to acknowledge the toast. "Skál" (pronounced "skowl"), which means "cheers" in Icelandic, is usual.

- Dietary considerations: If you have any dietary requirements or allergies, please notify your host or the restaurant ahead of time. Icelandic cuisine contains a variety of meals, including fish, lamb, and dairy items, so it is vital to express any dietary restrictions ahead of time.

- Finishing your dish: It is typically praised in Iceland if you complete the meal on your plate. It indicates that you loved the food and appreciated the work that went into making it. If you are unable to complete your meal, it is preferable to politely refuse extra portions rather than leave a substantial quantity of food on your plate.

- Conversation: It is usual in Iceland to engage in polite conversation throughout the dinner. Topics like Icelandic culture, nature, sports, and travel are typically safe to discuss and may help you connect with your hosts or other diners.

Remember that these are not hard and fast norms, and Icelanders are typically accepting of cultural variations. The most essential thing is to be kind, respectful, and grateful for the hospitality offered to you.

Chapter Eight

What To Know Before Traveling To Iceland

Arm yourself with important guidelines like a seasoned explorer before starting on an Icelandic journey. Knowing the ins and outs of this region of fire and ice may reveal hidden beauties and transform an ordinary trek into an incredible adventure.

The Icelandic currency

Iceland's currency is known as the Icelandic króna (ISK). Iceland's national currency is the króna, which is used for all financial transactions inside the country.

The Icelandic króna has the sign "kr" and the currency code ISK. Prices, for example, may be advertised as 1,000 kr or written as ISK 1,000.

Icelandic banknote denominations include 500 kr, 1,000 kr, 2,000 kr, 5,000 kr, and 10,000 kr. Coins are available in 1 kr, 5 kr, 10 kr, 50 kr, and 100 kr denominations.

It is important to note that Iceland maintains rather strong currency restrictions, which means that the movement of Icelandic króna into and out of the nation is limited. This is done to maintain the currency's and the country's economic stability.

It is best to exchange your money for Icelandic króna at a bank or currency exchange office while visiting Iceland. Credit and debit cards are generally accepted across the nation, and ATMs in most cities allow you to withdraw Icelandic króna.

Money Exchange Spot in Iceland

You may exchange money in Iceland at a variety of venues, including:

Banks: The majority of Iceland's main banks, including Arion Bank , and Landsbankinn, provide currency exchange services. They have locations in key cities such as Reykjavik, Akureyri, and Keflavik, as well as at the airport.

Currency Exchange Offices: Currency exchange offices may be found in important tourist sites and city centers across Iceland, notably in Reykjavik. They often provide affordable pricing and flexible operating hours.

Hotels: Some Icelandic hotels may provide currency exchange services to their visitors. However, the rates may be lower than those given by banks or specialist exchange offices.

Airports: The primary international gateway to Iceland, Keflavik International Airport, includes currency exchange facilities where you may exchange money upon arrival or before departure. Keep in mind, however, that airport exchange rates are often less attractive than alternative possibilities.

ATMs: You may also withdraw Icelandic króna (ISK) from ATMs using your debit or credit card. Even in tiny communities, ATMs are frequently accessible in Iceland. However, it's a good idea to verify with your bank ahead of time to confirm your card will function in another country and to question any fees or transaction restrictions.

To obtain the greatest bargain, examine exchange rates and fees before converting money. Also, keep in mind that credit cards are widely accepted in Iceland, and many establishments prefer electronic payment methods, which reduces the need for significant sums of cash.

LGBTQ + Acceptance

Iceland is largely recognized as one of the world's most LGBTQ+-friendly nations. Over the years, the nation has made considerable progress in terms of LGBTQ+ acceptance and equal rights. Here are some important aspects about LGBTQ+ acceptance in Iceland:

Legal Protections: LGBTQ+ people in Iceland have broad legal protections. Since 1940, same-sex sexual conduct has been lawful, and same-sex marriage has been permitted since 2010. Through a legislative decision, Iceland became one of the first nations to allow same-sex marriage.

Anti-Discrimination Laws: Iceland has strict anti-discrimination legislation in place to protect LGBTQ+ people from discrimination in sectors such as employment, housing, and public services. These laws guarantee that LGBTQ+ people are treated fairly and equitably.

Gender Identity Recognition: Iceland has progressive gender identity legislation. Transgender persons have been permitted to legally alter their gender marker on official papers without having to undergo surgery or sterilization since 2012. Individuals in Iceland may also pick a non-binary gender choice on official papers.

LGBTQ+ Rights groups: Iceland has various LGBTQ+ rights groups that campaign for the community's rights and well-being. These groups, such as Samtökin '78 (The National Queer Organization), seek to promote equality, give assistance, and increase awareness in the nation regarding LGBTQ+ problems.

Public Opinion: In Iceland, the majority of people favor LGBTQ+ rights. The majority of the population accepts and includes LGBTQ+ people. Pride festivities, like the Reykjavik Pride festival, are well-attended by both residents and tourists.

Icelandic politicians have shown strong support for LGBTQ+ rights. Many political parties publicly support LGBTQ+ equality and fight to put legislation in place that encourages inclusion and equal rights.

While Iceland has made tremendous progress toward LGBTQ+ acceptance, obstacles and incidents of prejudice may still occur. Overall, Iceland is regarded as a very LGBTQ+-friendly nation, with the rights and acceptance of LGBTQ+ people adequately protected by law and society.

Emergency Contacts

Here are some crucial contacts in Iceland in case of an emergency:

Dial 112 for emergency services.
In Iceland, this is the universal emergency number. It provides access to police, fire, and medical services.

Dial 112 for police.
You may also call the Icelandic police by phoning 444-1000 in non-emergency circumstances needing police help.

Dial 112 for medical assistance.
Dial 112 if you need emergency medical treatment or an ambulance.

Dial 1777 for Icelandic Roadside Assistance.
This number is just for roadside help, such as in the event of a vehicle breakdown or accident.

Dial 112 or 118 for the Coast Guard.
In the event of a maritime emergency, such as an accident or trouble at sea, call the Icelandic Coast Guard.

Call the Poison Control Center at +354 543 2222.
Contact the Poison Control Center if you have a poisoning emergency.

Dial 112 for tourist information and safety.
If you are a tourist in need of aid or information, contact 112 to reach the Tourist Information and Safety line.

While English is commonly spoken in Iceland, it may be beneficial to have a translation service or a local who can assist you if you are not proficient in Icelandic.

Iceland Cultural Etiquette

When visiting Iceland, travelers should be aware of the country's particular cultural etiquette. The following are some important features of Icelandic etiquette:

- Punctuality is crucial to Icelanders, so appear on time for planned appointments, meetings, or social

106

functions. Being late for no cause is considered impolite.

- Greetings: A forceful handshake and direct eye contact are customary when meeting someone for the first time. Icelanders may introduce themselves using their first names, and it is appropriate to do the same.

- Personal space: Icelanders usually value their privacy. When participating in conversation or socializing with people, keep an arm's length distance until they signal differently.

- Iceland is famed for its breathtaking natural scenery, and Icelanders have a strong appreciation for their environment. When exploring nature, it is important to stick to authorized roads and trails, avoid littering, and be cognizant of the ecosystem's fragility.

- Alcohol consumption: Although alcohol is allowed in Iceland, public drunkenness is frowned upon. Excessive drinking and loud conduct are not tolerated in public spaces. It is essential to drink responsibly and to follow local laws.

- Clothing: Because the weather in Iceland may be unpredictable, it's best to dress in layers and be prepared for changing circumstances. Casual wear is often acceptable in cities, although smart-casual gear is suited for more formal events or premium restaurants.

- Dining etiquette: It is usual in Iceland to wait for the host or the most senior person to begin eating before you begin. It's polite to eat everything on your plate since it shows you liked your dinner. It is also usual to express gratitude to the cook or host for the dinner.

- Politeness and directness: Icelanders are noted for their honesty and directness. They value open and direct communication, so it's often fine to share your thoughts and participate in open debates as long as you do it respectfully.

- Respect for local customs: Learn about Icelandic customs and traditions, such as the Yule Lads at

Christmas or the midwinter festival of orrablót. Display an interest in and respect for local traditions, and be willing to learn more about Icelandic culture.

Remember that cultural etiquette varies from person to person, so it's always a good idea to observe and adjust to the unique circumstances and people you meet while in Iceland.

Chapter Nine

Iceland Sustainable Budget Travel

Financial preparation and management are the compass and fuel that guarantee your trip to Iceland is both exciting and financially feasible.

Top Money Saving Strategies

Here are some great money-saving suggestions for travelers if you're planning a vacation to Iceland and want to save some money along the way:

1: Visit during the off-season: The summer months, especially July and August, are the busiest for tourists in Iceland. Consider traveling during the shoulder seasons (spring and fall), when lodging, airfare, and activities are often less expensive.

2: Book your rooms ahead of time: Booking your accommodations ahead of time will help you score better prices and prevent last-minute price increases. Consider sleeping in guesthouses, hostels, or campgrounds, which are often less expensive than hotels.

3: Cook your own meals since eating out in Iceland may be rather costly. Consider making your meals whenever feasible to save money on groceries. Many places to stay include community kitchens where you may make your own meals. Purchase items from grocery shops and local marketplaces.

4: Bring a reusable water bottle and refill it from the tap: Instead of purchasing bottled water, bring a reusable water bottle and refill it from the faucet. Iceland has plenty of clean and safe drinking water, so you can save money by not buying single-use plastic bottles.

5: Take advantage of free attractions: There are numerous free natural attractions in Iceland, such as waterfalls, geysers, and hiking paths. Plan your schedule to incorporate these free sites so you may take in the breathtaking natural beauty without paying a thing.

6: Use public transit or carpooling: Buses are a cheap method to get about Iceland, particularly if you're just going inside Reykjavik or between large cities. If you want to hire a vehicle, try joining a carpool with other tourists to divide the expense of gas and rental costs.

7: Consider camping: Camping is a popular choice in Iceland and may be a less expensive alternative to standard lodging. There are several campsites around the nation that provide minimal amenities and magnificent views at a fraction of the cost of hotels.

8: Look for discount cards or passes like these: Check to see if any discount cards or tickets for attractions, transit, or activities are available in Iceland. The Reykjavik City Card, for example, provides free admission to several museums, swimming pools, and discounts on a variety of businesses.

9: Take advantage of duty-free shopping: If you're traveling into Iceland, you may shop duty-free at the airport. You may save money on wine, cigarettes, and other items since they are often less expensive at duty-free shops than in conventional retailers.

10: Investigate and plan ahead of time: Planning ahead of time for your vacation will help you uncover the greatest offers, discounts, and inexpensive solutions. Look for online travel forums, blogs, and websites that provide money-saving advice and suggestions from other Iceland visitors.

Remember, although saving money is vital, don't forget to prioritize your safety and fun throughout your Iceland vacation.

Bargaining and Negotiation Strategies

When haggling and negotiating with market vendors in Iceland, it's crucial to remember the country's cultural standards and etiquette. Here are some pointers to assist you efficiently handle the negotiation process:

1: Research and comprehend the market: Before engaging in negotiations, acquire knowledge about the market and the things you want to purchase. This will provide you with a better grasp of usual rates and allow you to make a more acceptable offer.

2: Approach talks with courtesy: Icelanders appreciate courtesy and respect. Maintain a warm and respectful demeanor while negotiating. Being extremely assertive or argumentative may be seen as unfriendly.

3: Begin with a reasonable proposal: Begin the negotiation with a realistic and fair opening offer. This demonstrates that you have done your homework and are ready to participate in a productive conversation. Starting too low may be viewed as impolite.

4: Prepare to compromise: Bargaining is a two-way street, and both sides must be ready to make concessions. If the seller makes a counteroffer, thoroughly analyze it and be willing to change your expectations. Finding a happy medium is critical.

5: Be patient and persistent: Negotiations may be time-consuming, so be patient and persistent. Keep in mind that this is a dialogue about achieving a mutually beneficial deal. Don't hurry the process or become irritated if things don't go your way right away.

6: Use nonverbal communication: Body language is important in negotiations. Maintain eye contact, employ open, relaxed body language, and demonstrate genuine curiosity. This may aid in the development of rapport and the creation of a favorable environment for negotiation.

7: Keep in mind the local customs: Icelanders are famed for their honesty and sincerity. However, it is still necessary to exercise caution and be alert of possible frauds or counterfeit items. Before concluding the transaction, confirm the legitimacy and quality of the things you're interested in.

8: When talks reach an impasse or the seller refuses to meet your fair offer, it may be time to consider walking away. When you demonstrate your readiness to quit, the vendor may rethink their stance.

Remember that negotiation techniques differ across people and firms, so be adaptive and polite throughout the process. Following these suggestions can increase your chances of a successful negotiation in the Icelandic market.

Iceland's Top Budget Markets

Iceland is recognized for having a somewhat high cost of living in comparison to many other nations, as of my knowledge cutoff in September 2021. I can, however, supply you with information on several budget-friendly markets in Iceland that you may visit:

Bónus: Bónus is an Icelandic inexpensive supermarket chain. They provide a large variety of food goods at reasonable costs, including fresh fruit, dairy products, meat, and home staples. Bónus has many sites around the nation, making it convenient for budget-conscious buyers.

Krónan: Another low-cost grocery chain in Iceland is Krónan. They sell food, home goods, and personal care items, among other things. Krónan has multiple locations around Iceland, making it easy to purchase on a budget.

Netto: Netto is a budget grocery chain with locations across Europe, including Iceland. They provide reasonable rates on food and home supplies. Netto has many sites throughout Iceland and is a popular alternative for low-cost shopping.

Flea Markets: There are several flea markets in Iceland where you may find second-hand things, vintage goods, apparel, and accessories at inexpensive costs. Kolaportid and Gufunes market are two prominent flea markets in Reykjavik. These markets may be a terrific spot to look for one-of-a-kind finds.

Farmers' Markets: Iceland is well-known for its fresh vegetables and farming. Visitors to farmers' markets, like the one in Reykjavik, may buy fresh, locally produced fruits, vegetables, and other items directly from farmers. While costs may vary, farmers' markets may allow you to support local producers while also enjoying reasonable and high-quality items.

Please keep in mind that the availability and cost of certain items and marketplaces may have changed. It's always a good idea to verify current information or contact local sources for the most up-to-date information about budget markets in Iceland based on your travel dates.

Chapter Ten

Goodbye, Iceland

Farewell, Iceland; may your natural marvels continue to inspire and astound those who have the opportunity to see your majesty.

Favorite Travel Souvenirs in Iceland

Here are some of the most popular tourist souvenirs that people like bringing home from their journeys. Here are a few suggestions:

1: Local Handicrafts: Look for one-of-a-kind handcrafted goods that symbolize the region's culture and customs. Local artists might manufacture ceramics, textiles, woodwork, or artwork.

2: Consider acquiring traditional apparel or accessories such as a kimono from Japan, a poncho from Peru, or a kilt from Scotland. Alternatively, you might choose local-style accessories such as jewelry, scarves, or caps.

3: Local Food and Beverages: Bring back a flavor of the place by buying local chocolates, spices, teas, wines, or spirits. These are excellent presents for friends and family, as well as a way to preserve your trip's memories.

4: Souvenir Magnets or Keychains: These little, affordable things may be a fun way to remember your trips. Look for designs that use prominent sights or destination emblems.

5: Postcards or Prints: Collect postcards or prints of renowned locations or gorgeous vistas from your travels. To preserve your vacation memories, frame them or put them in scrapbooks.

6: If you like music, try purchasing a traditional musical instrument or local music CDs that reflect the spirit of the destination's music culture.

7: Collectibles: Each place has its own set of collectibles. Matryoshka dolls from Russia, tiny Eiffel Towers from Paris, or traditional African masks, for example. These may be used as display objects.

8: Local Literature or literature: Look for literature on the area's history, culture, or local tales. It's a terrific opportunity to learn more about the place and continue studying after your vacation.

Remember that the finest memento is one that has a particular value to you or is related to your vacation experience. Choose something that speaks to you and evokes happy recollections of your travels.

Safety Tips For First-Time Visitors

When planning your first vacation to Iceland, it's critical to emphasize safety to guarantee a safe and pleasurable experience. Here are some safety advice for first-time Iceland visitors:

Weather Conditions: The weather in Iceland may be unpredictable and change quickly, so always check the forecast before venturing out. Prepare for high winds, rain, fog, and temperature dips. Dress in layers and bring windproof and waterproof clothes.

Road Safety: If you want to hire a vehicle and travel across the nation, get acquainted with driving legislation and road conditions. Stick to established routes, particularly if you're unfamiliar with gravel roads. Drive carefully, obey traffic laws, and be aware of potentially dangerous weather conditions.

Save emergency contact numbers on your phone, including the Icelandic emergency line (112). It is the main number to dial in the event of an emergency, whether medical, search and rescue, or police-related.

Nature Hazards: Iceland has beautiful landscapes, but they may be dangerous. Stick to the established pathways and avoid cliffs, hazardous terrain, and glacier regions unless accompanied by a skilled guide. When visiting coastal locations, pay attention to tidal patterns to prevent being taken off guard.

Water Safety: Iceland is home to numerous stunning waterfalls, rivers, and hot springs. While they are tempting for a dive, it is essential to proceed with prudence. Keep an eye out for warning signals, avoid getting too near to waterfalls, and be wary of possibly powerful currents or rapid changes in water depth.

Nature and animals should be respected: Iceland is noted for its diverse ecosystems and wildlife. Show environmental sensitivity by avoiding littering, keeping on approved trails, and not disturbing animals. During the breeding season, keep a safe distance from animals, particularly seals and birds.

Stay Informed: Keep up with local news and safety warnings, particularly those about weather conditions, road closures, or other possible risks. Follow the advice of local governments and visitor information centers.

Inform Others: Make someone aware of your trip intentions and schedule, particularly if you want to visit isolated places. Inform your friends, relatives, or your lodging provider of your intentions. This manner, in the event of an emergency, someone will know where you are.

Travel Insurance: Having comprehensive travel insurance that covers medical emergencies, trip cancellation, and personal possessions is highly advised. Check that your insurance coverage expressly covers the activities you want to participate in, such as hiking, glacier excursions, or other adventure activities.

Follow any specific restrictions or instructions offered by local authorities or tour operators, especially while visiting protected areas or partaking in activities like camping or trekking. These standards are in place to protect Iceland's natural beauty while also ensuring tourist safety.

Remember that safety should always come first while visiting any place. You may have a wonderful and safe trip in Iceland if you take measures, keep educated, and follow local standards.

Helpful Websites and Bookings Resources

There are various useful websites and booking options accessible when it comes to organizing a vacation to Iceland. Here are a few examples:

Visit Iceland (*https://www.visiticeland.com/*): Iceland's official tourist website gives detailed information on the country's attractions, activities, lodgings, and events. It's a terrific place to start when organizing your vacation.

Booking.com *(https://www.booking.com/)*: Booking.com is an online travel agency. Booking.com, a popular website for booking lodgings, provides a broad selection of alternatives in Iceland, including hotels, guesthouses, flats, and hostels. It gives you the ability to compare costs, read reviews, and make bookings.

Airbnb: *http://www.airbnb.com/* Airbnb is a popular site for locating unusual lodgings such as flats, cottages, and even traditional Icelandic homes if you choose to stay in such places. It enables you to book directly with local hosts.

Iceland Guide (*https://guidetoiceland.is/):* This website provides a variety of vacation packages, guided tours, vehicle rentals, and a wealth of information about famous Icelandic places and activities. It's a useful tool for arranging your trip.

Car Rental Firms:

Reykjavik Cars (*https://www.reykjavikcars.com/):* Provides a large range of rental cars at reasonable pricing.
Blue Car Rental (*https://www.bluecarrental.is/):* Offers a selection of well-kept automobiles for touring Iceland.
Budget *(https://www.budget.is/):* A well-known automobile rental business with locations around Iceland.

The Icelandic Meteorological Office *(https://en.vedur.is/)* provides the following information: This website includes current weather predictions, traffic conditions, and other useful information for visitors visiting Iceland. It is important to check the weather forecast before embarking on any excursion.

Iceland Inspired (*https://www.inspiredbyiceland.com/*): This website provides information on Icelandic culture, local tales, and travel advice. It's a fantastic resource for vacation planning and uncovering hidden treasures.

Before making any arrangements, remember to read the reviews and compare pricing on other sites. Furthermore, for the most accurate and up-to-date information, it is always a good idea to examine official websites and government resources.

Conclusion

Finally, Iceland is a nation of fascinating beauty and stunning scenery that will make an indelible effect on every visitor. Iceland, with its breathtaking waterfalls and towering glaciers, geothermal marvels, and rocky coasts, provides a one-of-a-kind and awe-inspiring experience like no other.

We have studied the many areas of this magnificent country throughout our travel guide, revealing hidden jewels and must-see places. We dived into the Icelandic people's lively culture and rich history, uncovering rituals and mythology that provide an added layer of enchantment to the already stunning surroundings.

Iceland has something for everyone, whether you are an adventurer looking for adrenaline-pumping activities like glacier hiking and ice cave exploration, a nature enthusiast hoping to witness the mesmerizing dance of the Northern Lights, or simply someone looking for a peaceful escape surrounded by unspoiled nature. Remember to protect and maintain the natural beauties that make Iceland so distinctive as you begin on your Icelandic adventure. Take the time to explore the pristine landscapes, meet the friendly natives, and enjoy the slower pace of life that Iceland has to offer.

Iceland has become a favorite destination for tourists from all over the globe due to its easy transit infrastructure, high-quality hotels, and variety of fascinating activities. This book has supplied you with the essential knowledge to create a genuinely unforgettable journey, whether you're planning a short break or a longer excursion.

So pack your bags, fix your eyes on the country of fire and ice, and be ready to be fascinated by Iceland's unique beauty. Discover its mysteries, marvel at its marvels, and make memories that last a lifetime. Your Icelandic trip begins right here!

Printed in Great Britain
by Amazon